MAN'S SEARCH
FOR A
MEANINGFUL
FAITH

□□

ROBERT C. LESLIE

GRADED PRESS
NASHVILLE, TENNESSEE

MAN'S SEARCH FOR A MEANINGFUL FAITH

A study book

Copyright © 1967 by Graded Press

A publication of The Methodist Church prepared by the General Board of Education through the Editorial Division and published by Graded Press, the curriculum publishing department of The Methodist Publishing House, 201 Eighth Ave. So., Nashville, Tennessee 37203. Printed in the United States of America.

Unless otherwise noted Scripture quotations are from the Revised Standard Version of the Bible copyright 1946 and 1952 by the Division of Christian Education of the National Council of Churches, and used by permission.

Robert C. Leslie is professor of pastoral psychology and counseling, Pacific School of Religion, Berkeley, California.

Henry M. Bullock is editor of church school publications, Editorial Division, Methodist Board of Education. Horace R. Weaver is editor of adult publications. Harold L. Fair is editor of Foundation Studies in Christian Faith, the series of which this book is the first volume.

TO PAULA
CONSTANT COMPANION IN THE SEARCH

CONTENTS

EDITOR'S INTRODUCTION

The book you are now reading is the first *study book* in a new curriculum series, Foundation Studies in Christian Faith. A new part (or unit) will be issued three months from the publication of this part and for each succeeding three months over a two-year period. The remaining seven parts are described on the inside front cover of this book. The series—Foundation Studies in Christian Faith—therefore is an eight-part study that will run for two years.

The components. There are three "components" to each part of the study:

—the study book (which you are now reading)

—the book of selected readings

—the resource packet for leaders of adult groups

These three components make up one part. Each three months a new study book, a new book of selected readings, and a new resource packet for leaders of adult groups will be issued. The three components in each quarterly part have the same title. For example, the book of selected readings and the resource packet to accompany this book are also entitled *Man's Search for a Meaningful Faith.*

The study book. As you turn through this study book, you will notice several distinguishing features. At the beginning of each chapter are two or three suggested Bible readings. Read these in your Bible before you read the chapter. We recommend the *Harper Study Bible, Revised Standard Version* (published by Zondervan Publishing House) for home use by every member of the class. (Available from Cokesbury.) You will notice that asterisks (*) appear in each chapter, usually in connection with reference to a book, play, or poem. When you come to an asterisk (*), turn to the end of the chapter. There you will find the notes, which give the source of the quotation or reference.

Leadership procedures. You will notice as you look through this book that certain paragraphs have a small black square (■) at the beginning. These procedures suggest a wide variety of ways of reacting to the ideas raised in the material. It is not expected that a group will use every suggestion or procedure. The procedures are placed in the study book to encourage each member of the group to assume responsibility for discussion and to stimulate thinking as you read the book. There is no separate book for leaders. Leaders and other members of the group should each have personal copies of the study book and the book of selected readings. Only the designated leader or "teaching team," however, will receive the resource packet described below for use with the group.

The book of selected readings. Each person in the group should have a copy of the book of selected readings with the same title as this book, *Man's Search for a Meaningful Faith*. In the book of selected readings, you will find a wide variety of selections from a number of other printed resources relevant to man's search for faith. While it is not absolutely essential for every person to have a copy of the book of selected readings, the study will be significantly enriched if this study book and the book of selected readings are read and used together. They are companion volumes. Many procedures involve use of selected readings. In this study book you will frequently see the abbreviation *S/R* followed by a number. When you come to a place in the text where this abbreviation appears, turn to the book of selected readings and find the reading whose number corresponds to the one following the abbreviation *S/R*. The book of selected readings has no page numbers—rather, the selections are numbered. Reading and discussion of these selections will greatly stimulate study of this unit. Persons in the group who obtain all eight study books and all eight books of selected readings will have a basic library of the Christian faith.

The resource packet. In addition to a new study book and a new book of selected readings each three months, a resource packet for leaders will be issued, having the same title as the study book and the book of selected readings. These packets will contain a variety of resources for use by the leader with the group: filmslips, records, pictures, maps, charts, and the like. The packet will also contain a leaders' guide to suggest how the materials in the packet may best be used with the group. Each person in the group should have a study book and a book of selected readings; but only one packet will be needed for the group.

Covenant groups. Individuals in each group may wish to make a covenant with one another regarding this study. In this covenant, each person would agree to read the books faithfully in preparation for each discussion session and to be faithful in attendance and participation in the group meetings. Some covenant groups may wish to work out an agreement each person would be asked to sign; other groups may make the pledge without a formal agreement.

Leaders. The success of this two-year study depends in large measure on the leadership of the group. Some groups may wish to have a different leader with each new part of the study. Other groups may wish to divide each part, so that one person or couple takes responsibility for one or more sessions. Each person in the group should realize that faithful preparation and participation are essential if the goal of the study is to be achieved. The designated leader alone cannot and should not take the sole responsibility for the outcome of the study; this responsibility must be shared by all members

9

of the group. The group should become a community of study. (Selected Reading [abbreviated hereafter *S/R*], 1.)

Imagination. Groups who approach this study with imagination will find that the study may go on longer than the thirteen weeks of a quarter of the year. Do not feel that this study *must be* completed in three months. Your group might wish to extend the study to a longer period. Some chapters may be combined for one discussion session, others expanded to more than one. The series may be used in many settings other than on Sunday mornings. Use of the imagination will add liveliness and interest to the search for faith. For instance, if your church has a drama group, you might suggest that it produce one of the plays mentioned by the author in the study book. The use of music, art, and other resources will make the search for faith more meaningful.

Acknowledgments. This series—Foundation Studies in Christian Faith—is the work of many hands. There is not sufficient space here to name all those who have contributed to it. Harvey H. Potthoff, professor of Christian theology, Iliff School of Theology, led the subcommittee of the Curriculum Committee that· conceived this study. The following persons are due special thanks for their work on the project: Henry M. Bullock, editor of church school publications, and Horace R. Weaver, editor of adult publications, Mary Alice Asbury, Harold D. Minor, Nellie Moser, Lon A. Speer, and Judith Weidman, all staff members of the Editorial Division, Methodist Board of Education; William B. Bosworth, William H. Jackson, Dan Brawner, and Richard E. Elliott of Central Production Services; and Thomas K. Potter, Jr., manager of Graded Press, of The Methodist Publishing House. Thomas B. Newton, director of Central Research, The Methodist Publishing House, has made significant contributions in helping the editorial staff gain an accurate understanding of Methodist adults. To Robert S. Clemmons, staff member of the Division of the Local Church, Methodist Board of Education, goes credit for the concept of a study book correlated with a book of selected readings.

Most of the art reprinted in this book is from the collections of the Art Institute of Chicago, Chicago, Illinois, to whom we acknowledge with appreciation permission for its use. All photographic art is by Edward Wallowitch. We also gratefully acknowledge the permission of publishers whose credits appear at the end of the chapters to quote from the works cited.

HAROLD L. FAIR

AUTHOR'S PREFACE

This book is about man's search for faith—why he searches; the goal of his searching; the disappointments he finds in his search; the joy he experiences as he senses movement toward the goal of his searching and a better understanding of himself.

Though the search for meaning in our time is often not identified in religious terms, I take the position in this book that any search for meaning in life is a search for God—even though God may never be mentioned.

Out of my years of experience as a minister of The Methodist Church, trained in psychology, experienced as a chaplain in mental hospitals, and now teaching in a theological school, I have tried to understand how our minds and thoughts work as we search for faith. Because my own life's work has been so closely related to psychology, I see the search for faith most clearly in its psychological manifestations. This does not mean, of course, that psychology tells us all we need to know about the search for faith; but it does mean that psychology can bring significant insights into how we search for faith and how we sometimes make mistakes in our search. I am certain that psychology can be of great help to us in our search. Even before we can concentrate on the search, we must have some understanding of ourselves; and it is here that psychology has most to offer. The reader should notice, however, that throughout this book the insights of psychology are closely related to the Christian faith. This book is not about the search for any faith; it is about the search for Christian faith. The Christian faith provides the goal: commitment to the spirit of Christ; psychology helps us understand how we search and how we fail in the search.

The book is organized around the stages of life as set forth by Erik H. Erikson in several of his works. He has carefully studied the development of persons throughout life. According to Erikson, at each stage of life there is a particular need that must be met if maturity is to result. Each need, however, continues throughout the life span. Alongside each need a particular strength emerges. These emerging strengths provide the framework for this book. Chapter 2 stresses hope; successive chapters deal with will power, purpose, competence, fidelity, love, care, and wisdom. Throughout the book, the reader will notice the close relationship between emotional development and spiritual growth.

To assist the reader in seeing each topic related to his own life, I have introduced a fictional married couple, Archibald and Imogene. A twenty-four hour period in the life of Archibald provides continuity throughout the book.

Because some of the most profound searching for meaning is found in the modern theater, I have referred to a number of contemporary plays. In working with theological students, with young people, and with adult classes, I have found that the dramatist of today quickly involves people in his search even though he seldom offers easy answers. It is my hope that this book, the first of the Foundation Studies in Christian Faith, will involve its readers in a similar way in their own search for meaning, in their own search for God.

ROBERT C. LESLIE

Pacific School of Religion
Berkeley, California

13

Mark 10:17-22
A rich young ruler searches for meaning. (*S/R*, 2.)
Hebrews 11:1 through 12:2
The roll call of the faithful.
(*Read these selections in your Bible.*)

1

□□

WHO SEARCHES FOR MEANING?

Most of the time Archibald was a happy man. Now and then, however, he felt pretty discouraged. This had been one of those days. Nothing had gone right all day. The boss had been upset. The office staff had been restless. The job had seemed pretty dull. The traffic had been extra heavy coming home, and he had been late for supper. The children had fought at the table. Even Imogene, his wife, had been worried about repairs for their house. He hadn't had a moment's peace. And now it was bedtime.

■ One procedure for each chapter suggests that your group set goals. To help you get started, the study committee or leadership team might pose a question that, on the basis of its study and planning, expresses the main concern of the chapter. Now, as a group, ask yourselves: (1) What should we learn to help us answer this question? and (2) What should we do after we have found the answer? By your answers to these two questions, you will have set your goals

■ *In the room where your group is meeting, display a large poster on which are written assignments for specific preparation to be made by the members of the group before the session begins.*

15

for learning both content and behavior. Go through these steps as you begin the study of each new chapter, using a guiding question appropriate to the chapter.

Looking at himself in the mirror as he brushed his teeth, Archibald saw an anxious-looking man of thirty-eight, still youthful in appearance but beginning to show the signs of middle age. He knew he would feel better after a good night's sleep, but he couldn't help wondering if something basic was wrong. Had he really found what he was looking for in life? Was he fooling himself with his religious interests? Could there be more meaning in life than he had discovered?

A newspaperman leaves his reporting to sail alone in a tiny sloop across the Atlantic. A teen-aged boy from a good home joins a delinquent gang. A housewife struggles to become creative, but she complains that she is only marking time. A brilliant student drops out of college. A lawyer joins a free-dom march. A professor confesses that "God is dead."

Each of these persons is a normal individual, yet each senses that something is wrong. Each is striving to find more meaning in his life. Each is on a search. (*S/R, 3*.)

To search for meaning is nothing new. There is the famil-iar story of a rich young man who came to Jesus asking, "What must I do to inherit eternal life?" It is the story of a man who had nearly everything—but found no satisfaction in what he had. If he were to ask his question today, it would more likely be, "What must I do to find meaning in daily life? How can I get out of the rut in which nothing really seems to satisfy me? How can I live the kind of life that would be worth living forever?"

■ Introduce the idea that the search for meaning is not new nor is it always successful, by having one person read aloud the story of the rich young ruler (*S/R, 2*). Then let another person read aloud *S/R, 3*. (Has everyone in the group read the editor's introduction at the front of this book?) Each person think silently for one minute: The faith of the rich young ruler was not strong enough to meet the crisis facing him. Is my faith strong enough to handle a crisis like loss of all material possessions, or bereavement, or amputation?

■ Four persons, out of sight of other class members, read aloud "What If This Should Happen to You?" (Resource Packet, item 1). After hearing the readings, each person think silently: Do I need to search for a more meaningful faith?

■ Write, on a 3 x 5 card, an honest evaluation of the present state of your faith. Keep the card for use with Chapter 12.

We will be considering together in this book the struggles of many who are searching for meaning. Some are authors, writing books and plays about the search for meaning. Others are scientists, trying to find meaning in their laboratories. Most are ordinary people, sometimes finding partial answers, sometimes only meeting discouragement. Now and then, however, we come upon those who have found their answer through a religious pathway. How faith can help us to meet our needs and direct us to a more meaningful life is the aim of the book. How the persistent concerns of life can best be met through an informed Christian faith is the focus of our study.

MANY ARE SEARCHING

Archibald knew that he wasn't the only one who was searching for something. He recalled an article in *Life* magazine telling of Robert Manry. Manry was a forty-seven-year-old newspaperman who, in June, 1965, sailed in a tiny thirteen-and-a-half foot sloop from Falmouth, Massachusetts, to Falmouth, England. It took him seventy-eight days, alone on the Atlantic. Why did Manry do this? Perhaps it was because his life was in a rut, a routine that seemed rather senseless. He wanted to experience something more in life. He was looking for something more than he had found.

Robert Manry was not alone in his search. (*S/R,* 4.) A teen-aged boy who grew up in a nice suburban community joined a delinquent gang in the city. Telling how he became a delinquent, he said: "This way of life, I was convinced, gave me what I wanted, including purpose and meaning." He wanted more in life than he was finding. He was expressing some of the boredom he was experiencing.

17

Recently when I asked a middle-aged housewife how things were going for her, she answered in these words:

> If you mean, am I busy, yes, between a full-time job and several family crises in the past few years my time has been well occupied. If you mean am I doing anything particularly creative, no, I feel like I am marking time.

Housewives are not the only persons who feel they are marking time. A reporter tells of going to an exclusive college in the Northwest. This college has the reputation of accepting only the very finest students. The reporter was sent there by *Life* magazine to try to discover why so many students dropped out. He discovered that the reasons for dropout had very little to do with failure in study. As he puts it, "The real reasons come out when conversations in the dormitory shift around to 'What does it all mean?' and 'What's the use of it all?' " So the reasons for drop-outs in college have more to do with an absence of meaning in life than they have to do with failure in study.

The search for meaning is found in an acute form in the civil rights struggles. The bus boycott in Montgomery, the "freedom rides" to Jackson, the freedom marches in Washington and Selma, the riots in Chicago, San Francisco, and Atlanta were all a part of the effort of the Negro community to gain access to a world of greater meaning. It is not surprising that students and others all over the country, both Negro and Caucasian, have responded to the efforts by joining the demonstrations. Whether the demonstrations have taken place in crucial centers of struggle or on university campuses, they reflect the striving of concerned persons for equal opportunity for all people in housing and employment and in the courts. Many a young person has found meaning for himself as he has helped others in their search. (*S/R*, 5.)

Another evidence of the search for meaning is found in the "God is dead" idea. Several young professors are using this figure of speech to make it clear that the image of God held by many is outdated. They insist that a childlike understanding of God is no longer appropriate in the complex

18

atomic age. To assert that God is dead is to declare that much of our religious thinking about God needs to be revamped in order to see God as really essential for life. Thus the religous world, too, is caught up in the search for greater meaning. (*S/R,* 6.)

This search for meaning is being emphasized in a number of unexpected places. There is a new mood, for example, in the science of psychology. During the years between 1946 and 1955, when many former servicemen were involved in graduate study in psychology, new questions were being asked. The questions were: "What does it all mean?" and "Why am I here?" These questions indicated a longing, a hope that somewhere in the social sciences answers could be found to the question of meaning. (*S/R,* 7.)

More and more patients are complaining to their doctors of a general sense of dissatisfaction, of an absence of any sense of meaning. (*S/R,* 8.) Increasingly, psychological counselors are looking at the larger, more general problems centering in the lack of meaning than they are in specific symptoms.

One such therapist is psychiatrist Viktor Frankl who, like Freud, is also from Vienna. Frankl uses the term *existential vacuum* to describe a feeling of inner void, of inner emptiness. He often finds this feeling among his patients. Many psychiatrists are finding more and more patients who complain of a lack of a sense of meaning, who are without purpose, and who speak of a sense of futility about life. Such, for example, was a forty-year-old junior college professor. He was successful as a teacher and was popular with his students. Nevertheless, he sought treatment because he felt that he was leading a completely meaningless kind of life. He had achieved success in the eyes of the world but was unhappy and discontented within.

■ As a whole group, share examples of this ongoing search for meaning evident in the news reported by radio, television, and newspaper. *S/R,* 4, 6, and 8 illustrate this search.
■ Divide the group into pairs. Give each pair a recent popular magazine. Using the following guidelines, let each pair study the various advertisements and select two to interpret to the class.

What deep-felt personal needs does the advertised product or plan claim to satisfy? How would satisfaction of that need add meaning to a person's life?

Show how advertisements indicate that the search for meaning may differ according to a person's age, sex, marital status, and profession.

As these ads are shared, you may wish to group them on a bulletin board according to the various needs.

SOME AVOID THE SEARCH

Sometimes Archibald wondered if he were foolish to try to find more meaning in life. Many of his fellow workers made fun of him when he asked them questions about what they were living for. Most of them seemed too busy even to stop to talk about life. Sometimes he felt that Imogene's busy schedule was an escape from thinking deeply. And many of his friends were occupied with so many activities that they ran from one thing to another like overactive teen-agers, never even thinking about the meaning of it all. He had a feeling that some kept going because they didn't like to face the answers waiting for them. He knew that others were too involved in getting money or achieving power or struggling for happiness to even bother with thinking about meaning.

Most people are like Archibald's friends. Occasionally, however, someone asks the question about meaning. A cartoon in a current magazine shows a businessman, dressed for work, returning from the railroad station instead of going to work. The wife is shown at the door, still in her bathrobe, with a cup of coffee in her hand and a perplexed look on her face. Her husband says, "I reached the station, bought my paper, saw the train approaching, suddenly asked myself 'Why?', got into the car again, and came home." (S/R, 9.) The cartoon is funny because so few businessmen ever actually ask questions about the meaning of what they are doing.

Elizabeth Barrett Browning wrote of people who are too preoccupied with minor concerns to be interested in the great issues of life. Her lines refer to the biblical story of the call of Moses to a position of leadership. According to tradition, God spoke to Moses out of a burning bush which was not consumed. Mrs. Browning writes:

> . . . Earth's crammed with heaven
> And every common bush afire with God;
> But only he who sees takes off his shoes,
> The rest sit round it and pluck blackberries.*

■ Discuss in the total group: How do *I* escape asking, What is the meaning of life? Why is it difficult to face the question? What demands on us might call forth a response like that given by the rich young ruler in *S/R, 13*? What answers could you give if you, like the man in the cartoon (*S/R, 9*), asked yourself, "Why?"

Some in our own time turn from any significant search for meaning because clear answers are hard to find. People are easily upset when clear-cut answers are not ready when needed. We like to be certain even though the day of absolute certainty has almost disappeared.

Arthur Miller has written a play called *After the Fall* in which the chief character is a middle-aged lawyer named Quentin. The play consists of flash backs into Quentin's life as he thinks over the events that have brought him to the present moment. In the opening scene Quentin summarizes the mood of many middle-aged persons in our day. He looks up at the bench in the court where the judge usually sits only to find that the bench is empty. An "empty bench" where there is "no judge in sight" is a way of saying that specific answers, definite judgments, are lacking.

Arthur Miller is skillful in presenting modern man's problems. Like most contemporary authors, he is not a religious man in the usual sense of the term. But he *is* deeply religious in the profound sense of the word. All of his plays deal with basic moral issues. And in all of his plays the issues are handled in terms of personal choice. It is finally the individual who chooses how he will live and how he will die. Without using religious language (indeed, he offends some people with his forthright frankness), Miller deals with great religious concerns of life. (*S/R, 10*.) In *After the Fall* he struggles, like many other modern writers, with the questions that confront

21

man in his search for meaning. The title of the play refers to the Adam and Eve story, the "fall" from innocence. Miller sees hope for man only when he recognizes his fallen state, when he accepts his inclination toward evil. When man gives up his certainty about his own goodness, hope begins.

It is not easy for many of us to give up the sense of certainty. Many of us are like Maggie and Louise in *After the Fall*. Both these women had been married to Quentin. One of Quentin's complaints about them was that they had been so arrogantly sure about everything. Well, the day of absolute certainty is gone. The man of the future is the man who can live with uncertainty, with ambiguity. A man can no longer train for a single vocation with the expectation of spending his life in one narrow speciality. The rate of change is so rapid today that a man can expect to do two or three different kinds of work before his working career comes to an end. Just when life seems certain and secure, change is likely to erupt. (*S/R*, 11.) For the rich young ruler, the drastic change from a thing-oriented world to a person-oriented world was more than he was willing to attempt. "His face fell and he went away with a heavy heart . . ." (Mark 10:22, New English Bible) .

Even if one does not fear change, the search for meaning is not always welcomed. Some believe, for example, that it is unhealthy to search for meaning. Freud once wrote: "The moment a man questions the meaning and value of life, he is sick." Followers of Freud up to the present have tended to ignore meaning and value as inappropriate concerns in the struggle for health. In the Freudian tradition, more emphasis is placed on life experiences in the past with special reference to ineffective patterns established very early in life. Conflicts of adult life are less concerned with where a person is *going* than with where he has *come from*. By clearing up the unresolved problems of the past, the possibility for future growth is much greater.

Others, however, hold an opposing point of view. One such person is Viktor Frankl. Frankl does not think a person is sick or abnormal when he questions the meaning and value of life. He says that a man who questions the meaning of life "only proves that he is truly a human being." Frankl recognizes that the search for meaning is upsetting, that it is difficult and not always rewarding. But he also asserts that it is the clearest distinction between a human being and an animal. To raise questions is to act like a person is supposed to act! (S/R, 12.)

Frankl tells about treating a seventeen-year-old girl. Although the girl sought help for a problem with her heart, Frankl helped her most in her search for meaning. She wanted to find reasonable answers to her questions. She was troubled over not finding a clear sense of meaning. Her boyfriend ridiculed her search for more than mere pleasure in life. Frankl emphasized the human quality of her search:

> Who searches for meaning? Certainly an ant will not, neither will a bee. A girl, however, of 17, posing such questions and involved in such a quest proves to be a truly human being struggling for meaning. . . . You are right in contending that pleasure cannot be the main thing in life. Struggling for a meaning in life, at the risk of foundering in the search with questions and even doubts, is not only normal during puberty but is even the prerogative of youth. A truly young person never takes meaning for granted but dares to challenge it.*

The search for meaning is a good sign. Wherever Jesus sensed any openness in a person to explore the deeper levels of meaning, he took advantage of it. When the rich young ruler asked about what he needed to do to obtain eternal life, Jesus understood his request to be a longing for answers to the perplexing unanswered questions of his life. Although the young ruler wasn't very good at asking the right questions, his dissatisfaction with his life was obvious. Jesus interpreted a willingness to discuss the meaning of life as an openness to growth. He encouraged people to search.

SOME SEARCH WITH FAITH

As Archibald dropped off to sleep, his last waking thoughts were pleasant ones. He didn't "say his prayers" as he had been taught as a boy, but he did feel a warm sense of thankfulness for his family. Lying beside Imogene he felt very much at peace. Their physical expression of love was very satisfying to him. The children were asleep; the house was quiet. He wasn't sure what lay ahead for him and for his family, but he felt confident that things would work out. He hadn't always felt that way. Marriage had helped, and especially marriage to Imogene. Feeling more confident on the job had helped. Feeling more able as a parent had also helped. God was a part of it, too, although he couldn't say just how. He remembered the words of a Christmas card which appealed to him:

> And I said to the man who stood at the gate of the
>   year:
> "Give me a light, that I may tread safely into
>   the unknown!"
> And he replied:
> "Go out into the darkness and put
>   your hand into the Hand of God.
> That shall be to
>   you better than light and safer than a known way." *

Archibald wasn't sure what it meant to put his hand into the hand of God—but at least it suggested that there would be help in finding his way.

A part of the tragedy in the life of the rich young ruler was that he couldn't accept the invitation of Jesus to become one of the disciples. In that choice company he could have been supported in his search for a new pattern of life. Jesus did more than just challenge him to get rid of the things that stood in the way of personal relationships. He offered the opportunity of fellowship: "Come, follow me." But the rich young man couldn't risk a break with the patterns that had brought such financial security. Having sought meaning through the acquiring of things, he could not risk seeking meaning in persons. His faith was not strong enough to witness to it through such a radical change. (S/R, 13.)

Joseph Conrad has a short novel called *Heart of Darkness* which is an account of a journey into the dark depths of a man's life. In this story a river boat breaks down far up a river in the Congo and needs some major repairs. Marlowe, the hero of the book, is trying to make the repairs. He is terribly frustrated. Although he has the plates that are needed to repair the body of the ship, he has no rivets at all. He discovers that the plates, by themselves, are worthless. Religion can be thought of as being that force in life that takes individual experiences and rivets them together into a meaningful whole. (S/R, 14.)

In the popular play by Thornton Wilder called *Our Town,* Wilder describes how the trivial, everyday events in life contain the deepest meaning. He tells of a letter received by little Jane Crofut from her minister when she was sick. The letter was addressed to Jane Crofut at her farm in New Hampshire and included town, county, state, continent, hemisphere, and planet, ending with "the mind of God."

It is as if the playwright were saying that whatever goes on in your life and mine, even in the ordinary activities of life, is not unrelated to the mind of God. It is part and parcel of our relationship to God. Howard Thurman says it this way: "Man comes into the presence of God with the smell of life upon him." When we are talking about searching for a meaningful faith, we are not talking about a dimension of life that is special and different and set apart from ordinary life. We are talking about what happens to your life as you sit here in this group. We are talking about what happens in your life as you leave the church building or other group setting and go to your home. We are talking about what takes place in your life in this day. (S/R, 15.) You find your way into a meaningful relationship to life not in some special adventure but in adding the dimension of depth to the ordinary, everyday events of life.

Of course, some people find meaning in their lives in extraordinary circumstances in life. I recall, for example, talking with a social worker in Berlin about the days of the airlift. You will remember that the city of West Berlin was supplied entirely by air during the winter of 1948 and 1949. Two million people had all of their supplies flown in. The winter was very cold that year. Like most Europeans, the social worker heated her apartment with a coal stove. But of course there wasn't any coal to be had. The only fuel she had was provided by the American newspaper that the armed forces put out. After she had finished reading the paper, she would take each single sheet, wad it up in a tight little ball, and use it for her fuel. When she had burned each of these pieces of paper, there was no more fuel until the next day. Every morning she would have to break the soap away from the basin where it had frozen during the night. There was never enough food. She would wake up at night feeling the familiar pangs of hunger and sensing the tension of anxiety until she heard overhead the sound of the transport planes. The sound never stopped except when the weather was impossible.

The social worker went to the theater and watched the performance in candlelight. Since there were no streetcars running, she had to walk through the dark streets—no lights, of course. Those were years in which all the normal comforts of life were denied. And yet, as she talked about those years, she said: "Those days were the greatest days of my life."

I suppose most of us would say that we find the greatest meaning in life when things are comfortable and convenient and when we have all the luxuries of life around us. Yet here was a woman who affirms that the period of greatest meaning for her came in the days when all the luxuries of life were denied. (S/R, 16.) I had the feeling that she longed for the return of those days. She went on to explain why. She said: "In those days we knew that we had to demonstrate to the Russians that they could not break our spirit." She found a meaning for her life.

Religious faith makes its contribution by pulling a person out of himself and relating him to something bigger than he is. Or perhaps it helps him to sense that the ordinary routine events of life are related to something that is much bigger. When Jesus objected to the rich young ruler calling him "good," he may have meant that goodness is not something that can be added to a life by the observance of certain laws or the carrying out of certain rituals. Goodness is a matter of how a person's total life is oriented. The problem with the rich young ruler was that his life was so totally oriented in the wrong direction. He was so thoroughly oriented to things that he had lost sight of people. He had to make a clean break from the world of things before he could begin to find meaning. He had to change his emphasis from things to persons.

When persons are central, anyone's world expands. Among European peasants, it is the custom to do homage to anyone who has died, whether he is known or not. As a funeral procession passes by, the peasant takes his hat off and stands in reverent silence. He knows, in the words of the English preacher-poet John Donne, that he is "involved in mankind." The poet makes his point clearly: . . . "Never send to know for whom the *bell* tolls [when someone has died]; It tolls for *thee.*" * What touches any man, touches every man.

In the final analysis, a person's faith compels him to think of his life in broader terms. How do you feel when you go to church? Does it help you in your personal search for meaning? Going to church always says to me that my search is never large enough, that the interests surrounding my life are too small. The cross reminds us all of the larger and deeper dimension in life.

Have you ever thought of religion as being the dimension of depth? Most of us think of religion as being one dimension alongside of many others. This is to say that there are the areas of work, of vocation, of intellectual interests, of study. And there are the areas of social life, of recreation, of religious life, of worship. According to the late Paul Tillich, the religious dimension in life is not one along with others, not one area of life on a parallel with others. But it is any dimension of life pursued in depth. You can start with any area but as you carry it into depth you find yourself dealing with the religious dimension. (*S/R*, 17.)

27

When considered in terms of the dimension of depth, Arthur Miller's *After The Fall* is a religious play. He starts dealing with relationships between a husband and a wife, but before he finishes he is dealing with the question of trust and forgiveness. He starts dealing with the friendship between two men, but soon is facing the question of the meaning of loyalty and commitment. He starts dealing with the fact of a death in a family but then struggles with the question of how reality can be faced. The dimension of depth is present in all the ordinary events of life, but it needs to be discovered. (*S/R*, 18.) Life lived in faith, life lived in the presence of God, is life lived in the dimension of depth.

Life lived by faith has still another characteristic. It is life lived with a fundamental optimism. It is an optimism based on a conviction that this is God's world and that in God's world there is a way through difficulties. This optimism is expressed vividly in an inscription in a little chapel in England called the Chapel of Staunton Herald. The words were written at the time of the Cromwell Rebellion when the future of the country seemed very uncertain. No one knew quite what to expect. But one man at least dared to affirm his faith:

> In the year 1653 when all things sacred were throughout ye nation either demolished or profaned, Sir Robert Shirley, Barronet, founded this church; whose singular praise it is to have done the best things in the worst times and hoped them in the most calamitous.

To do the best things in the worst times and to hope them in the most calamitous is characteristic of the person who, in his quest for meaning, sees his life firmly rooted in a relationship with God.

■ Show the filmslip, "Search" (Resource Packet, item 2). Suggestions for using the filmslip and questions for discussion appear in the Leaders' Guide in the packet.

■ Let three persons engage in a panel discussion as follows: (A panel consists of three to six persons who talk together before an audience about an assigned topic. A moderator will introduce the subject and keep the conversation moving and pertinent.)

One person will discuss religion understood as the dimension of depth (pages 27-28). See also *S/R*, 15.

A second person will discuss Tillich's idea of the depth dimension (*S/R*, 17).

A third person will discuss the analysis of the dimension of depth as seen in *After the Fall* (page 28).

Then all members of the panel may join in discussing, How do I see faith, understood as the depth dimension of all of life, as a help in my search for meaning?

■ Discuss in the total group: Do we find greatest meaning when life is most difficult? If so, why? If not, why? How important to me is the search for a meaningful faith? React to ideas presented in Chapter 1, through the panel discussion, and in the Selected Readings you have read.

■ Close the session by praying together the "Prayer of Saint Francis" (Resource Packet, item 3).

■ You may want to set a date now and begin making plans for a TV or theater party as suggested in the procedures in Chapter 10.

NOTES ON CHAPTER 1

Page 21: From "Aurora Leigh" by Elizabeth Barrett Browning.

Page 23: From an interview recorded in lecture-demonstration, Vienna, Spring, 1961.

Page 24: From "The Gate of the Year" by M. Louise Haskins in *Masterpieces of Religious Verse,* edited by James Dalton Morrison (Harper and Row, 1948), page 92. Used by permission of Charles L. Wallis.

Page 27: John Donne, *The Complete Poetry and Selected Prose of John Donne* (Random House, 1957), page 441. Used by permission.

John 4:4-29
A Samaritan woman longs for meaning. (S/R, 19.)

Jeremiah 31:31-34
The new covenant in the heart.
(*Read these selections in your Bible.*)

2

□□

DARING TO TRUST

Archibald groaned as the alarm clock woke him from a sound sleep. It was never easy to get up in the morning. The day loomed ahead of him like a demanding taskmaster. He could never quite appreciate Imogene's cheeriness in the early morning. She always jumped out of bed as if she were glad to greet a new day. She often sang as she dressed. As for him, the minutes between hearing the alarm and leaving for work were the worst part of the day. Somehow it was always hard to get started. A cup of hot coffee helped, but something deeper was involved. It was as if he couldn't trust himself to what the day might bring.

Getting started in a new day is a problem for many. Archibald is not alone in his dislike of the early morning hours. To face a new day with optimism calls for more than a good night's sleep. It calls for a genuine attitude of trust, for a confidence about what the day will bring forth and about how it can be handled. It calls for a feeling of being "all right," of

---

■ *As you arrive at your place of meeting, check the assignment chart for specific preparation to be made before the session begins.*

31

being "O.K." It calls for a confidence about the world that sees life itself as "all right" or "O.K." (S/R, 20.)

The familiar story of the Samaritan woman at the well tells of a woman who did not feel "O.K." Her response to the friendly words of Jesus was one of pulling back, of expressing distrust. She could not believe that he was only being friendly. She tried to turn his simple request for a drink into an argument. Indeed, the very fact that she was at the well in the heat of the day (the Hebrew sixth hour being about noon) indicated something was fundamentally wrong in her life. The women normally gathered in the early morning. As the story develops, it becomes clearer that she was a person on the defensive. She did not trust anything that Jesus said but tried to argue with him. The trust with which he faced life was in sharp contrast to her attitude.

TRUST IS LEARNED

Archibald sensed that the difference between Imogene and himself was the difference between a person who could trust life and one who could not. He knew that Imogene could greet each new day confidently because she trusted life. He realized that he, on the contrary, tended to shrink from each new day because he could not feel certain about how things would turn out. He remembered his father criticizing him when, as a young boy, he had wanted to help in the basement workshop. His father had said to him more than once, "Leave the tools alone. You can't do anything right."

Neither Imogene nor Archibald could tell you why they feel the way they do, although they have some beginning hints about it. The Samaritan woman, too, would have been hard pressed to explain why she acted the way she did. The ability to trust has deep-seated roots. When a religious person tells of trusting in God, he is talking about trusting in life, because he sees all of life as lived under God. All the experiences that contribute to one's feeling about the world

32

contribute to one's thinking about God. These experiences begin very early. (*S/R*, 21.)

The most basic need in life is the need to trust. The trust the child develops toward his parents, and especially toward his mother, is the beginning of the trust he feels toward God in later life. When trust is absent, nothing else works very well. When trust in God is present, the parts of life tend to fall together into a unified whole.

The movie *David and Lisa* is the true story of two teenagers who, as patients in a school for emotionally ill young people, find their way back to health. Both have withdrawn from life into a fantasy world because neither can trust anyone else. Each has developed a way of warding off the world, of creating a private world of fantasy. But both are miserable in the isolation of their own creation. The story develops around their efforts to establish contact again with the real world through establishing a relationship with each other.

David, the boy, has created for himself a world largely free from any personal relationships. By concentrating on mathematics and physics, by playing chess and doing mechanical drawing, David creates a world that he can treat as a kind of mechanical model. In this world of unchangeable law he does not need to function like a person. He does not need to have feelings, to feel alive as a person, to enter into a relationship with others. Indeed, he refuses to have any physical contact with anybody. He runs from the touch of a person as one might run from danger. He protects himself by staying out of contact with people.

Lisa, the girl, handles her problem in a very different way. She talks only in rhyme. Whereas David refuses physical touch, Lisa refuses ordinary conversation. By withdrawing into a special world in which everything rhymes, she builds a kind of fortress to protect herself from a threatening world. It is as if she is saying that her spirit has been broken by contacts with the everyday world, so she has retreated into a special world of her own making. Unable to trust the world as she finds it, she creates a peculiar world in which she can feel more secure.

Unable to trust people at large, David and Lisa are able to trust each other when each has respected the other's defense. In the final scene of the movie, Lisa is able to talk without rhyming and David invites her to take his hand. As they walk hand in hand, the miracle performed by trust has taken place again, and both are well on the road to health. (*S/R*, 22.)

The covenant of trust, however, is not easily formed by those who have been hurt in life. Although we have very few facts about the Samaritan woman, we can easily believe that promiscuous relationships with men were a substitute for entering into relationships of real trust. Jesus did not hesitate to point out the moral problem in her life. There could be no real happiness, no genuine satisfaction in passing sexual relationships. Her real need was to learn to give herself in trust to lasting relationship. (*S/R*, 23.) Jesus' words to her were intended to help her develop that attitude of trust in God that seemed to be absent from her life. His statement to her that God was to be worshiped neither on the Samaritan mountain nor in Jerusalem suggests that Jesus was trying to help her see that the God who would be present in all of life could not be localized on any mountain. This God could be trusted. (*S/R*, 24.)

We see in David and Lisa an extreme form of a common situation. When people are unable to enter into relationships of trust, they develop ways of behaving that are often ineffective. But their behavior can be understood as attempts at self-protection. The basic need, of course, is not so much to change the behavior as it is to develop the capacity to trust.

The New Testament says very little about the childhood of Jesus. We can infer, however, that the home in which Jesus grew up was filled by trust in God. This trust in the home of Joseph and Mary helped Jesus from the very earliest years of his infancy to mature in trust in God. It was in this mood of trust that Jesus could face the cross. He did not want to die, but because his trust was so great, he could face death. As long as he felt he was doing God's will, he could handle whatever life would bring.

Such trust is first developed through relationships with people, especially with parents and other significant persons in early life. Because our experiences with people are constantly changing, our feelings of trust are changing, too. At first we trust in God because we have learned to trust in people. Then we learn to trust people because of our trust in God.

■ Set goals for your study of this chapter as suggested on pages 15-16.
■ Consider the effects of the absence of trust in the life of a first-century woman and in the lives of two young persons of the twentieth century.

Have two persons read, in dialogue fashion, the story of the woman of Samaria (S/R, 19). A narrator should read the introductory verses and the closing verses. Then let all persons read silently the summary of *David and Lisa*, pages 33-34.

Discuss in the total group: How is mistrust evident in the lives of these persons? When and how does trust replace mistrust for them? Evaluate the idea that you must learn to trust persons before you can trust God. S/R, 21 and 22 may help you here.

TRUSTING IS HARD

As Archibald struggled to come awake, he thought back to the days of his engagement to Imogene. They had been classmates in the same college and had eaten together in the college dining room. He remembered how he had always rushed from class to get to the dining room early so that he could save a place for Imogene. Imogene would saunter in at the last minute, confident that there would be a seat for her. She always had the feeling that things would work out. He seldom had that feeling, but he longed for it.

Many persons are like Archibald. Unable to feel supported by life, they carry an added burden of anxiety that makes every task a bit harder. They are like beginners who are trying to learn to swim. They haven't yet discovered that the water will hold them up if they don't fight it. With most of their energy devoted to thrashing around in the attempt to stay above water, they have little energy left to propel themselves forward.

The mood of mistrust is nothing new. The Samaritan woman's initial failure to respond to the approach of Jesus is typical of many today. (S/R, 25.) When trust has been placed in sex rather than in persons, the evidence is clear that trust in life itself is lacking. The playwright Tennessee Williams writes, "Things have a way of turning out so badly." * He is summing up a point of view that is common in the thinking of many. Amanda, the unmarried sister in *The Glass Menagerie,* who speaks this line, has actually retreated from life. She finds her only real delight in a collection of glass animals. She tries to build a life around a collection of things as a substitute for relationships with people.

A part of the appeal of TV "westerns" is that things always turn out so well. The hero and the villain are clearly identified. The hero always wins and the villain is always defeated. There is no question in the mind of the viewer about the outcome. In a world in which, for many, things turn out so badly, the TV world of "westerns" offers a temporary escape.

Contemporary plays, on the contrary, tend to stress the tragic facts of life. There are few fairy-tale endings with everyone living happily ever after. In attempting to describe life as it comes to many, modern playwriters tend to portray characters who have lost the capacity to trust. When Arthur Miller ends two of his most successful plays with suicides, he is making an observation about current life. In *Death of a Salesman,* Willy Loman makes a god out of success. When he fails as a salesman, he sees nothing left for him but suicide. In *All My Sons,* Joe Keller devotes all his efforts to building a business to leave to his sons. By allowing inferior workmanship to go undetected, he is responsible for the loss of many lives. When his betrayal of moral standards is discovered, he kills himself. Both men had lost the capacity to trust; both had sought to support themselves in immoral ways. Both undermined hope.

Willy Loman tries pathetically to find his hope by a return to the good old days:

> . . . How do we get back to all the great times? Used to be so full of light, and comradeship, the sleigh-riding in winter, and the ruddiness on his cheeks. And always some kind of good news coming up, always something nice coming up ahead. . . .*

In contrast to the great times of the past, Willy sees his life in the present "ringing up a zero." His tendency to turn back to the past is like that of the Israelites in the biblical story. Threatened by uncertainties of the future, they pleaded to return from wandering in the wilderness to the security of life in Egypt, even in slavery.

It is easy to become discouraged by the problems that loom ahead. (S/R, 26.) It is hard to trust in one's capacity to handle life. Spies were sent by Moses to spy out the Promised Land. When they brought back a pessimistic report of "a land that devours its inhabitants" and of people that looked like giants, many of the Israelites wanted to turn back. Their plea was, "Would it not be better for us to go back to Egypt?" (Numbers 14:3).

If all one can see in life is sound and fury and if life has no more sense than is found by an idiot, there is not much reason to hope. If the future is empty, "signifying nothing," there is not much reason to press on into the future. This was really the mood of the Samaritan woman. When the woman said to Jesus: "Give me this water, that I may not thirst, nor come here to draw" (John 4:15), she was really expressing a longing for a change from a meaningless life. A paraphrase would convey an idea such as this: "Give me water that I need not keep coming in this dreary drudgery, day after day, to draw water in the meaningless routine of everyday existence."

To build hope back into a life that has lost hope is no easy task. The David and Lisa story is an important one because it helps to show how hard it is to break down a "security operation" that is a defense against anxiety. Lisa's rhyming and David's withdrawal from human touch were patterns used as protection against further hurt. They were attempts at making themselves feel more secure. The return of David and Lisa to the point where they could trust each other enough to drop their protective devices was a long, slow process.

■ Study the picture "Ship in a Storm" (Resource Packet, item 4) while a member of the class reads aloud Mark 4:35-41. Contrast the fear of the disciples and the faith of Christ in this situation.

Discuss as a total group: How did Jesus teach his disciples to face trouble in life? How is it possible for us to experience trust either in God or in persons in time of trouble? What "security operations" or methods of self-protection do you make use of when you are anxious or unsure?

Read silently S/R, 24. How might this help you learn better to trust? See the Leaders' Guide for this item.

■ Enumerate, without discussion, reasons why it is difficult to trust persons and God. These might be listed on a chalkboard or on newsprint.

Discuss as a group: How do we feel and act when we can't trust God and persons?

Then listen as three persons read aloud, as dialogue, S/R, 26. Discuss the attitudes of the three characters. Where, if at all, is trust present? On what basis can J.B. make his affirmations about God? How does his attitude compare with that expressed in S/R, 25? How may we develop the capacity to look to the future with anticipation?

FACING THE FACTS

It wasn't the first time Archibald had struggled to get going. Sometimes it seemed to him that talking over his fears with Imogene made them seem less threatening. The problems never seemed quite so bad when he tried to put them into words. When he simply thought about them to himself, there never seemed to be any answers. But Imogene's confidence was contagious. Perhaps he needed to confide in her even more.

Archibald, of course, was only discovering what many persons have found: the first step toward really handling any need is to face it. From this point of view, the Samaritan woman had been helped to make a good start; she was facing the emptiness of her way of life. She wasn't able to put her problem into words, but she was trying. Her attempts at talking about eternal life had more to do with finding meaningful patterns in her current life than it had to do with life after death. In a life that added up to very little real satisfaction, she was trying to find some pathway of greater meaning.

To face things as they really are is the first step toward handling them. Problems have to be solved on the basis of the facts as they are.

Wishful thinking is an activity engaged in by most of us at one time or another. If only we were not so fat, or so clumsy, or so short, or so sickly. If only we had more money, or more power, or more brains, or more beauty. If only we had been born into another home, or at a different time, or in a different race. But all the wishful thinking in the world doesn't change the facts. Eventually we have to begin with the facts as they are given. (S/R, 27.)

Facing the facts turns out to be more possible than many believe. Although many do not realize it, the human being has an amazing capacity for living with reality but very little capacity for living with deception. The facts, when faced, turn out to be endurable, but living with deception leads to illness. In Arthur Miller's play *After the Fall,* Quentin and his brother, Dan, are faced with the problem of telling their father that their mother has died. Dan is afraid that the father will "fall apart," and so he wants to avoid the issue. But Quentin disagrees: "I can't agree; I think he can take it, he's got a lot of stuff. . . ." * When they do tell their father, his response is a very emotional one, but he handles it. Quentin summarizes the experience: ". . . Still, a couple months later he bothered to register and vote. . . . Well, I mean . . . it didn't kill him either, with all his tears. . . ." *

■ Facing the facts is the first step toward handling life. Read silently "Deniers of Reality" (S/R, 27). Think silently: What facts do I need to face about myself; about my capabilities; about my marriage or my singleness; about my job; about my future; about my relationship to God? What, if any, action shall I take? Three by five inch cards should be provided for all who wish to keep a written reminder of their resolutions or decisions.

A good deal has been discovered in recent years about dealing with grief. The ancient truth of the beatitude: "Blessed are those who mourn, for they shall be comforted" (Matthew 5:4), has been rediscovered. Encouraging mourning leads to comfort. The only way to handle grief is to face the sense of loss openly, to express the sorrow freely. (*S/R*, 28.) Those who are able to express their grief at the time of death are able to handle their loss more effectively than those who withhold such expression.

Evidence of the need for expressing grief has come from a study of mothers who delivered premature babies. This study reached the conclusion that there was a difference in the ways mothers reacted to the premature births. This difference accounted for the mother's emotional state. Whether or not the baby lived, some mothers went through the crisis with flying colors. Others were still suffering from the effects of the crisis many months after it was behind them. The difference lay in how the situation was faced. Those mothers who insisted on getting the facts, who plagued the doctors and nurses for more information, who continually called the hospital for progress reports, who talked and cried and acted out their anguish were the ones who made a good recovery. But those, on the other hand, who refused to face the facts, who made no inquiries, who withheld their sorrow, who wouldn't even talk about possibilities of life or death—they were the ones whose problem stayed with them for months. They carried the effects of their unexpressed anxiety into all other parts of their lives.

The leader of this research team gives some suggestions about how the mothers might have been helped.

If a husband had spoken of his fears for the baby . . .
If a friend, instead of sending an evasive "Get Well" card (as

if this were the problem!) had written, "We are thinking of you and hoping and praying that the baby will live. . . ."

If a doctor had spoken frankly . . .

If a neighbor had offered to go along to the hospital to see the baby, still in the incubator, still frighteningly small . . .*

The point is that the mothers needed help in facing the facts. They could handle their grief if first they could recognize and admit it.

When the mother was helped to face the facts and to live with them, she made good progress regardless of the presence or absence of inner character. Untrained persons can help in a crisis. Professional training is not required to help people face the facts as they are given by life. When the helping person can deal with the facts openly and in an attitude of trust, the person in crisis is encouraged to do the same.

■ Let everyone in the class read silently the section of the material that deals with grief (pages 40-41), or one member may report the main points of the section. Then have someone read aloud S/R, 28.

Role play (a spontaneous acting out of a situation to gain insight, to learn how others feel, or to solve a problem) a situation in which one person attempts to help a bereaved person. Try two approaches:

The helping person glosses over the facts, tries to make everything appear rosy.

The helping person talks honestly with the bereaved about the facts.

Discuss: How does each approach affect the development of trust?

TRUST REQUIRES COMMUNITY

It wasn't difficult for Archibald to understand Imogene's optimism. Her whole family had such a positive feeling about life that she could hardly be different. He knew that she often puzzled over his uncertainties about himself and the future. She was so sure that things would work out. It was as if her daily theme were expressed in the hymn she loved to sing:

This is my Father's world,
O let me ne'er forget

41

That though the wrong seems oft so strong,
God is the Ruler yet.
("This Is My Father's World," stanza 3.)

Archibald could not sing these words with conviction but he felt closest to their truth when he was with people like Imogene. His own sense of trust was strongest when he was with others who really lived in trust.

To replace mistrust with trust is never easy. The difficulty of reversing the process is well known to anyone who has tried. Those of us who have been blessed with the kind of loving family relationships in which trust is so natural that it is taken for granted have trouble recognizing how hard it is for some to learn to trust. (S/R, 29.)

The story of David and Lisa is taken from clinical records. It is the true story of two teen-agers who found their way back into the real world. But it is more than that. It is the story of how people grow out of mistrust into trust. It tells of a covenant established, a promise of faithfulness out of which growth can take place. It tells of the absolute necessity for human community in which love and trust have been established beyond question.

A similar theme is developed in the novel *Exodus*, the story of the founding of the new nation Israel. Seventeen-year-old Dov Landau was a product of the ghetto of Warsaw and of the concentration camp in Auschwitz. He was about as bitter and hardened as a human being could be, until he met Karen Hansen. Slightly younger than Dov, Karen took him on as her special charge. One day, as she was comforting a child in the detention camp,

she looked up and saw Dov standing over her. "Hello," he said very quickly, and walked away.

Despite the continued warnings of many to leave him alone, Karen knew she had penetrated a great darkness. She knew the boy was desperate and trying to communicate and that his "hello" was his way of saying he was sorry. . . . To everyone else . . . but Karen, Dov Landau was incorrigible. He spoke only in anger. She was always called upon to calm his sudden eruptions.

She saw in him things that no other person saw—wonderful strength and pride.*

In the presence of Karen's loving concern, Dov changed. In the community of trust which developed between them, his outer shell of defense gradually dropped away and the unique human being emerged. As the *Exodus* story unfolds, Dov becomes one of the heroes in the struggle to establish the new nation.

The idea of a community of trust is nothing new to the Christian faith. One of the fundamental concepts of the Jewish tradition out of which Christianity developed is the idea of covenant. A covenant is an agreement, a compact entered into by two parties. It is an agreement that becomes binding upon both. In the agreement certain obligations are accepted as the terms of the relationship. When the Pilgrims left Europe to seek freedom in a new land, they saw themselves as making a holy pilgrimage. Anchored in Cape Cod Bay, their first harbor in the new land, one of their first acts was to draw up the Mayflower Compact. In this document the following words occur: "We do solemnly and mutually in the presence of God, and one another, covenant and combine ourselves together. . . ." The first words of the Compact are: "In the name of God, Amen." Almost their first act in the new land was to assert the relation of covenant with God, to place themselves under God's guidance.

The idea of the covenant permeates the biblical faith. The biblical book of Exodus is the story of a people who covenanted with God, who established a relationship of trust with him. The covenant was a promise that called for responsible behavior on the part of both parties, of both God and the Israelites. God would give guidance to his chosen people, and they, in turn, would obey his laws. The Ten Commandments are an expression of the responsibility of man as a part of his promise. The constant concern of God for his chosen people is shown by the deliverance from slavery in Egypt and by the giving of his son in Jesus.

43

The concept of the covenant gradually changes from a promise to fulfill specific laws to a promise to live according to a God-like spirit. Jeremiah speaks of a new covenant characterized not by obedience to external law but by loyalty to an inner spirit.

> "I will put my law within them, and I will write it upon their hearts; and I will be their God, and they shall be my people" (Jeremiah 31:33).

In the Sacrament of the Lord's Supper, the ritual includes reference to the new covenant in these words taken from 1 Corinthians 11:25: "This cup is the new covenant in my blood." The new covenant is the new promise of trust and mutual love. The New Testament church is assured by Paul that the young Christians are no longer strangers to the covenant but are "fellow citizens with the saints and members of the household of God" (Ephesians 2:19).

Trust is not learned from a book; it has to be experienced in life. It comes best when it is a part of life from the start, when the child experiences it with his parents at the very beginning of his life. But it is not restricted to such experience. Trust can be discovered at any period of life and in the presence of anyone. It comes most often in communion with another person (as with David and Lisa) or in fellowship with other people (as with the disciples). It can come in our church groups, even in this study group. A member of a study group tells how he dared to begin to trust:

> "Specifically, the release for me in the group came when I realized (as I now see) that we didn't talk about basic Christian trust, but the group trusted me and the immediate trust is real. . . ." *

To begin to trust, one must be trusted!

The mood of the Samaritan woman at the end of the biblical story is that of hope. As was true in her life, hope develops out of trust. The person who can face the future in a hopeful mood is the one who has been helped to trust life.

Hope is an outgrowth of trust. Optimism about life, hope for the future, is directly related to the development of trust. The need to learn to trust is crucial for without trust there is little hope, and without hope there is little meaning. But when one finds that he is trusted, when one learns to trust, then he is in a position to begin to hope.

■ Divide the group into pairs. Review together the treatment of growth from mistrust to trust as seen in *David and Lisa* (pages 33-34) ; *Exodus* (pages 42-43) ; and the biblical covenant (pages 43-44) . Talk about times when you have actually experienced trust of persons and God.

Share with the entire group reasons why trust was possible for you.

■ Is your group developing the kind of trust that invites personal sharing and acceptance of what is shared? Read silently *S/R, 29.* Then in the light of this reading, individually evaluate your group using items C through H from *S/R, 30.*

■ Pray together the "Prayer of Saint Francis" (Resource Packet, item 3) .

■ Take the necessary assignments for through-the-week study.

NOTES ON CHAPTER 2

Page 36: Tennessee Williams, *The Glass Menagerie* in *Six Great Modern Plays* (Dell Publishing Company, 1958) , page 506. Used by permission of Random House.

Page 37: Arthur Miller, *Death of a Salesman* (Viking Press, 1949, page 127. Copyright 1949 by Arthur Miller. Used by permission of the publisher.

Page 39: Arthur Miller, *After the Fall* (Viking Press, 1964) , page 8. Copyright © 1964 by Arthur Miller. Used by permission of the publisher.

Page 39: *After the Fall,* page 11. Used by permission.

Pages 40-41: Gerald Caplan, *Principles of Preventive Psychiatry* (Basic Books, 1964) , page 290. Used by permission.

Pages 42-43: Leon H. Uris, *Exodus* (Doubleday and Company, 1958) , pages 164 and 166. Copyright © 1959 by Leon H. Uris. Used by permission of the publisher.

Page 44: Quoted in Philip A. Anderson, *Church Meetings That Matter* (United Church Press, 1965) , page 100. Used by permission.

Luke 15:11-32
The prodigal son comes to himself. (S/R, 31.)

1 Samuel 17:1-54
David kills Goliath with a slingshot.

Genesis 4:1-16
Cain struggles with sin.

(Read these selections in your Bible.)

3

□□

COMMAND THE MORNING

As Archibald drove into the city to work, his thoughts turned to his boss at the office. He admired the boss and wished he could be more like him. In fact, he tried to copy the boss's way of doing business with people. But it hadn't worked. Somehow the approach that worked so well for the boss didn't work for him. Trying to act like the boss had made him feel uncomfortable, unnatural. He had finally decided that he would have to be himself, that he would have to develop his own approaches. But he wasn't really sure what his own natural way was. And how could he be sure that he was on the right track? How could he really know himself?

Self-discovery is one of life's most persistent problems. The biblical story of the Prodigal Son is a great story because it centers on the need for self-discovery. In the words of Luke's gospel, the younger brother "came to himself." Up to

■ *As you arrive at your place of meeting, check the assignment chart for specific preparation to be made before the session begins.*

that point he hadn't been his real self. He had only been the part of himself that was in rebellion. He had been driven by the need to separate himself from his father and from his father's standards, but then his real self took over. He made his own choice. He took himself in hand and began to direct his own life. He found himself as he began to exercise control over his life. (*S/R,* 32.)

BEING AN INDIVIDUAL

As Archibald struggled to be his own unique self, he realized that his self-image was not very clear. He had been a part of a large family where there never seemed time to give attention to the individual child. His brothers and sisters seemed more talented than he was. They seemed to have a clearer idea about goals in life than he had, and they seemed more confident about achieving them.

Imogene had this same confidence. Sometimes Archibald wondered if she wasn't too certain, too confident. She wasn't always accepting of weakness when she found it in other adults. She knew so little about weakness herself. But he knew about it. He saw himself as always uncertain, never really sure about anything. He had so many doubts about himself. He knew that he did not come through as a strong person. But he wanted to very much.

The struggle to be an individual is often a lifelong concern. Some, like the Prodigal Son, discover themselves only through acute suffering. More are like the Prodigal's older brother who did not experience life through crisis but rather through slow growth in normal routine. Some choose to hide their individuality since being an individual means accepting personal responsibility. Yet, everyone yearns to be treated as a person in his own right. (*S/R,* 33.)

The need to be treated like a unique person is a consistent theme of life. Quentin's wife, Louise, in *After the Fall* says to her husband, "I am a separate person!" * She has been saying that Quentin wants her to surround him with praise, but she insists she can't do that. She wants to be herself, not just a support for him.

> "Look, Quentin, . . . you want a woman to provide an . . . atmosphere, in which there are never any issues, and you'll fly around in a constant bath of praise. . . .
>
> . . . .
> Quentin, I am not a praise machine! I am not a blur and I am not your mother! I am a separate person!" *

When Quentin asks Louise what it means to become a separate person, her answer is: "Maturity." * One of the marks of being an adult in a mature (fully grown) sense is certainly the sense of being a unique, separate person. The steps leading to maturity in a Christian sense are quite easy to define, but hard to attain. The first step is to see oneself as different from others and appreciated for the difference. Seeing oneself as a child of God is to feel liked in one's individuality. It is to feel accepted by God even though one is aware of much in himself that is unacceptable. It is out of this acceptance that one is able to reach out in accepting ways to others. Christian maturity involves the kind of self-appreciation that makes possible a forgetting of self in relationships with others. Feeling loved by God, the Christian expresses his love by reaching out in love to others. Maturity thus always involves feelings about oneself and others. (*S/R, 34.*)

■ Set goals for your study of this chapter as suggested on pages 15-16.

■ Have one member of the class read aloud the story of the Prodigal Son (*S/R, 31*) as other members of the group study the picture in the study book, page 46.

Allow time for silent self-analysis. As you continue to study the picture, answer the following questions for yourself: If God is represented by the father in the picture, how do you see your relationship to God—like the Prodigal Son or like the elder brother? In what sense might you need to "return to the father"? Do you see yourself as generally acceptable or generally unacceptable? Can you accept forgiveness? How do you come to terms with yourself each day? Read *S/R, 32*. How does your self-understanding improve your sense of personal worth? Look at *S/R, 33*.

As the group remains in the spirit of quiet self-examination, one member of the class will read aloud *S/R,* 34.

There is something very appealing about a person who is his own self. In American culture, when a person is asked who he is, the customary answer comes first of all in terms of occupation ("I'm a carpenter, an accountant, a house-wife") and second in terms of group affiliations ("I'm a Methodist, a Democrat, a Caucasian"). It is refreshing to find a person who answers: "I'm me, I'm myself. I'm Imogene!" Such a person is free to be himself and doesn't need to take on the coloring of each different situation. (*S/R,* 35.)

The temptation to adopt the ways of others is a constant one. The novel by Sloan Wilson called *The Man in the Gray Flannel Suit* is the story of Tom, a rising young business executive. Tom, like "a half million other guys in gray flannel suits," * struggled to get ahead without violating his integrity. The temptation was very strong to say what the boss wanted him to say rather than to be honest and speak the truth. Tom put the problem very neatly: "How smoothly one becomes, not a cheat, exactly, not really a liar, just a man who'll say anything for pay." * (*S/R,* 36.) Prodded by his wife, however, he decided to speak the truth and did so even though he realized he risked his job. Later he talked it over with his wife:

"I needed a great deal of assistance in becoming an honest man. If you hadn't persuaded me to play it straight with Ralph [the boss], I would be thinking differently now. By a curious coin-cidence, Ralph and a good deal of the rest of the world have seemed honest to me ever since I became honest with myself. . . . I'm sure things are going to be better. I've become almost an optimist." *

When people can be honest with each other, things *do* go better. Carl Rogers, one of the best-known workers in the counseling world, testifies to the importance of honesty and of genuineness in counseling relationships. "The most im-portant ingredient," he writes, ". . . is that I should be real."

To be real, for him, means to be genuine, the opposite of being phony. He goes on to describe how being real helps:

> *In my relationship with people I have found that it does not help,*
> *in the long run, to act as though I were something that I am not.*
> It does not help to act calm and pleasant when actually I am
> angry and critical. It does not help to act as though I know the
> answers when I do not. It does not help to act as though I were
> a loving person if actually, at the moment, I am hostile. It does
> not help for me to act as though I were full of assurance, if
> actually I am frightened and unsure.*

More and more we are discovering that a major task in counseling is to help a person to express his own unique self. (S/R, 37.)

The principle of genuine encounter between persons is, of course, much broader than a counseling technique. Paul Tournier, a Swiss psychiatrist, writes from a point of view of biblical faith. He tells of the contributions made to his life by his wife and by his friends who were open and frank with him. He goes on to say:

> In my turn I saw that by adopting a more personal tone myself
> I was helping others to become personal, not only in my consult-
> ing room, but in the most ordinary conversation in the street, on
> military service, or in a medical conference. And I realized how
> men thirst for the real contact, from which new life springs up to
> blow like a fresh breeze among us and within us.*

Tournier's point of view is shared by a great many. People crave genuine relationships that are so hard to find in an impersonal, industrialized culture. (S/R, 38.)

■ Pretend that all persons in your class are strangers to one another. Let each person write on a 3 x 5 card a brief identification
or introduction of himself. Collect the cards and have them read
aloud. As they are read have someone keep count of the number
who identified themselves in the way suggested on page 50. How
do you react to the idea of introducing oneself as, "I'm me, I'm
myself"?
■ Divide the group into small groups. Read the excerpt from *The
Man in the Gray Flannel Suit* (S/R, 36). If you were, or in fact are,
in Tom's dilemma, how would (do) you handle these thoughts:
   "I should quit if I don't like what he does . . ."

"I'll always pretend to agree, until I get big enough to be honest without being hurt."

"I'll be tactful . . . I'll not be rude enough to say a stupid speech is stupid. How smoothly one becomes, not a cheat, exactly, not really a liar, just a man who'll say anything for pay."

What choices other than quitting or agreeing might Tom have? What are some of the ways in which we daily suppress our individuality and become "a man who'll say anything for pay"? How can you speak the truth to persons without being destructive?

■ You may wish to show the filmstrip, *Members One of Another,* which deals with being a genuine self. It may be acquired from your conference board of education or from Cokesbury.

GAINING FREEDOM

Much as Archibald wanted to be free and open with his friends, and especially with Imogene, he did not dare to let go. He had so many doubts about himself, and he felt so ashamed of many of his feelings. Only rarely could he risk letting his real self show through. Imogene was different. You always knew just how she felt because she wasn't afraid to let her feelings come out. She seemed to trust her feelings. (*S/R, 39.*) She was relaxed not only in her attitudes about herself but also in her attitudes toward their children.

Imogene's trust in herself and in the world helped her to see herself as an individual in her own right. And she was especially good at helping their children to feel important as persons. Archibald recalled a scene in their home the previous Sunday as their little three-year-old daughter, Joan, was trying to get into her coat to go to Sunday school. Her little fingers weren't able to button up the coat. When he tried to help her she had insisted, "I can do it. I can do it myself." Imogene had stepped in then saying calmly, "Of course, you can do it. And Mummy will help you." Little Joan felt pleased, and the coat got buttoned! Imogene had combined parental help with a respect for her child's independent stirrings.

A combination of freedom and authority is necessary for a sense of individuality to develop. The story of the Prodigal Son combines the issues of freedom with authority. Because the younger son was first granted freedom, he was then able to accept his father's authority. He struggled in young manhood, however, with an issue that might have been resolved at a much earlier age.

A sense of individuality is crucial for feelings of autonomy to develop. Autonomy means "the capacity to direct one's own life, to exercise independent control." The autonomous person is essential for any democratic way of life. He is a strong safeguard against external control, whether it comes from a dictator or from a pressure group.

A sense of autonomy is developed in countless ways in the home. One of my colleagues tells of planning his new home with the needs of his growing boys in mind. He had a very difficult time interpreting to the paper hanger that the cowboy wallpaper belonged in the master bedroom. The paperhanger could hardly understand parents who chose a modest bedroom for themselves and designed the more spacious room for their children. Here were parents who showed respect for their children's needs in the very architecture of their home! The boys could hardly miss the message: their needs counted. It wasn't that they were more important than their parents. The point was that their needs at the moment called for the larger room.

Most of us who are parents find it difficult to remember that the child's feeling of personal significance develops in many small ways. I am always interested in where adults play games with children. Most children will sit on the floor to play Chinese Checkers or to build with blocks. The parent who insists that the game be played on a table is requiring that the child fit the parental mode of life. Or consider how we celebrate a season like Christmas. I recall taking my children into the city to see Santa Claus when both of the youngsters were quite small. The city, itself, was quite a new experience for them, let alone the ferry boat trip across the bay, followed by the San Francisco cable car ride. I took them to see Santa Claus, but it wasn't easy to drag them away from the escalator, the moving stairs. As I look back on the occasion now, I realize that a visit to Santa Claus was very much an adult idea (and quite a confusing one to the young child). But stairs that moved! This was something really special, something close to their experience. They had enjoyed climbing up and down stairs for some time, but they had never before seen stairs that moved! Were I to make that trip again, we would forget the adult Santa Claus and would concentrate on the idea of a good time. For out of such attitudes the child's idea of his personal significance develops.

A former student at Stanford University recalls an experience in which he was helped to feel important. As a freshman, he was approached on the campus by the distinguished president of the university, David Starr Jordan. As he pondered whether or not it was appropriate for a lowly freshman to speak to the president, Dr. Jordan quietly tipped his battered hat. The student discovered that this was Dr. Jordan's common practice. Later he learned that Jordan tipped his hat to every student because students were people with potentialities. The president expected them to go places!

Some are denied exposure to people like Dr. Jordan and have to prove their capacities to themselves. They have to discover themselves. The Prodigal Son was such a person. His story of wasting his substance in riotous living becomes clearer in the light of a recent news clipping. In a story about the use of drugs on campus, one coed who was interviewed on the Berkeley campus in the San Francisco area spoke as follows:

> First I came to Berkeley from L. A. [Los Angeles]. Then I pierced my ears. Then I went on a few marches. Then I tried pot [marijuana]. Then I lost my virginity. And soon, I'll probably try LSD. I think after that, I'll have done everything, and it'll be time to go home.*

For this girl, leaving home seemed necessary in order to try to discover what she was really like. She is a contemporary example of the Prodigal Son. She squandered her self. She felt she had to experiment with letting go of some of her standards learned from others in order to take on standards of her own. She wanted to find her own autonomy, to test her own capacity to handle life. She felt she had to discover that she was, in fact, free to make her own choices.

To be sure, there are many other more effective ways of establishing autonomy. In order to discover a feeling of personal importance it is not necessary to overthrow moral standards or to stand over against social custom. Many persons are helped in home and church and school to discover their own autonomy early. They do not need to rebel in defiant ways. Others deliberately set out to discover themselves through involvement in work projects in slum areas, through building projects in undeveloped communities at home and abroad, through participation in short-term missionary service or in the Peace Corps. (*S/R*, 40.) A single summer spent as a volunteer on the ward of a mental hospital or in voter education and registration or in a work camp in Mexico can do wonders toward developing a sense of personal identity and significance.

Being oneself rather than a carbon copy of someone else is essential for any kind of effective living. One of the great contributions of Christianity to world culture is the insistence of the Christian faith that every single person is important. How to help each person to *feel* important is one of the tasks of the Christian community. Involved in this task is the need for a person to love himself "properly," to use the fitting term of Rabbi Joshua Liebman. (*S/R*, 41.) A proper love of self is very different from a selfish, self-centered view. It is rather a fulfillment of the second great commandment set forth by Jesus: "You shall love your neighbor *as yourself*" (Matthew 22:39, italics mine) . That is, you extend to your neighbor the same kind of appreciation of him as an individual that you cherish for yourself. When self-love is proper, love for others follows naturally. (*S/R*, 42.) When self-love is lacking, the problem of loving others is never solved. Proper self-regard is essential for dealing with all authority questions. The most difficult boss is the one who really questions his own adequacy. The most rigid father is the one who is threatened when his authority is questioned.

The development of a sense of individual significance, a sense of individual autonomy, cannot be stressed too much. Most problems of prejudice center in a holding on to old ideas because of the fear of losing control if new ideas are introduced. (*S/R,* 43.)

A well-developed sense of autonomy is essential if one is to stand up and be counted in the presence of social injustice. The person who is not conformed to the world but who transforms the world is one who senses his own personal significance. (See Romans 12:1-2.) He sees himself as one capable of throwing the weight of his influence in directions of his own choosing. The question of autonomy is based in the struggle between freedom and autonomy. The autonomous person knows that he is free to make his own choices.

The story of the Prodigal Son might more rightly be called the story of the understanding father. The father let the younger son have his fling. He let the older son express his sense of injustice. He allowed both boys to choose their own patterns. He encouraged them in their autonomous striving. He did not attempt to dictate how they should live, but he was always ready to welcome them, with eagerness, as they sought a new relationship with him.

It is clear that Jesus is saying in the story in Luke 15 that God is like this father. He grants autonomy, welcomes experimentation, encourages freedom. When things go wrong, he welcomes the penitent. He does not wait at home to pass out punishment. He goes out to meet the wanderer with a glad hand and an open heart.

■ Development of individuality requires an environment of freedom and authority. Review the illustrations given in this section and read especially *S/R,* 40, 41, and 42. Discuss together: Why is it difficult for parents or adults to encourage freedom in children or youth? How can we achieve a balance between freedom and authority? How may involvement in service to others help one develop a sense of identity and personal significance? How can we distinguish between a proper love of self and a selfish self-centered view?

■ Look at the picture, "Who Bugs You?" (Resource Packet, item 5). See the Leaders' Guide for specific help in studying the picture.

Then divide into small groups to discuss questions such as these: In view of your sense of personal worth, how do you react to the authority figures in the teaching picture? What do your reactions reveal about your attitude toward freedom and authority?

AFFIRMING SELF-CONTROL

As Archibald drove along, he thought about the text his minister had preached on the previous Sunday. It was from the Book of Job, a book Archibald knew very little about. But the text had been a striking one: "Have you commanded the morning since your days began?" (Job 38:12). Archibald knew himself well enough to know that the text made an impression on him because he would have to answer: "No." Much as he wanted to, he often felt helpless about taking charge of his life. He so often felt pushed rather than feeling that he had chosen his path deliberately. With Imogene it was different. But she had a problem, too. Sometimes she was inclined to take over when she hadn't been asked.

A part of the appeal of the Prodigal Son story lies in the son's positive declaration: "I will arise and go. . . ." The Bible is full of similar affirmations. When the spies who had searched out the Promised Land brought back a negative report, Caleb stilled the crowd's reaction. "Let us go up at once, and occupy it; for we are well able to overcome it" (Numbers 13:30). But the people did not follow him. In a confidence similar to Caleb's, Gideon was able to lead his people into victory. "Arise," he declared, asserting that the Lord would give them victory (Judges 7:15). This same kind of personal decision is demonstrated in Daniel. He "resolved that he would not defile himself with the king's rich food" (Daniel 1:8). In each instance, a personal choice was made.

The degree to which a man is free to choose his own course of action has been a favorite theme throughout literature. It is one of the persistent questions of life. The novelist John Steinbeck deals with this theme in one of his greatest novels,

East of Eden. In the novel a contemporary family relives the story of Cain and Abel. Adam Trask has two sons, Caleb and Aron. Like the biblical Cain, Caleb feels that his brother is favored over him by their father. In *East of Eden* Caleb does not kill his brother, as Cain killed Abel. But he has many of the same angry feelings toward him. Eventually Caleb plays a part in the events that lead to Aron's death. In the biblical story, Cain's punishment was to be "a fugitive and a vagabond in the earth." He was sent out of Eden and "dwelt in the land of Nod on the east of Eden." * (See also Genesis 4:8-16.) Through the lips of Lee, the servant-companion, Steinbeck says:

> "I think this is the best-known story in the world because it is everybody's story. . . . I think everyone in the world to a large or small extent has felt rejection. And with rejection comes anger, and with anger some kind of crime in revenge for the rejection, and with the crime guilt—and there is the story of mankind. . . ." *

Steinbeck is interested in more than the story of rejection and the crime that easily results out of anger. The Cain and Abel story *is* the story of mankind because it deals with how man handles sin. Steinbeck notes that in the biblical record there is a sentence that can be translated in several ways. In talking about how sin always is lying in wait, "couching at the door," the record goes on to say: "But you must master it" (Genesis 4:7, Revised Standard Version). In the King James Version of the Bible, these words are a promise: "Thou shalt rule over him." In the American Standard translation, rather like the Revised Standard Version, the words are an order: "Do thou rule over it." But the Hebrew can still be translated another way. The word *Timshel* can mean "Thou mayest rule over him."

Here suddenly is a whole new way of thinking about sin, for here is the declaration that man has a choice. Steinbeck puts his thoughts again in Lee's words:

". . . There are many millions in their sects and churches who feel the order, 'Do thou,' and throw their weight into obedience. And there are millions more who feel predestination in 'Thou shalt.' Nothing they may do can interfere with what will be. But 'Thou mayest'! Why, that makes a man great, that gives him stature with the gods, for in his weakness and his filth and his murder of his brother he has still the great choice. He can choose his course and fight it through and win." *

This kind of writing shows how some of our ablest authors draw upon the biblical heritage. When Steinbeck wants to wrestle with the question of man's capacity to exercise choice in a way that distinguishes him from an animal, a biblical story provides the background. Here is a novelist helping to clarify a theological idea. Steinbeck is no stranger to the church. In his account of a tour he took across the country and back, he writes that he attended church every Sunday, visiting a different denomination every week. In his preface to *East of Eden* he suggests that his story is one that touches on good and evil, pleasure and despair, joy, gratitude, and love. His subjects are the subjects of the Bible, the subjects of life itself. His message in the novel comes through very clearly: man is free to decide how the circumstances of life will affect him—even the circumstances of the most awful kind of sin.

A characteristic of man is that he chooses how he will handle life. The Prodigal Son says to himself, "I will arise and go. . . ." He is asserting the natural posture of man— erect, head held high, facing the future. Psychiatrist Viktor E. Frankl in the 1940's survived two and a half years in four different concentration camps. He tells of how so many who died in the camps "entered those gas chambers upright, with the Lord's Prayer or the *Shema Yisrael*" * on their lips. Frankl insists that the freedom of choice can never be taken away from man:

He is free—free "from" all conditions and circumstances, and free "to" the inner mastery of his destiny, "to" proper upright suffering. This freedom knows no conditions, it is a freedom "under all circumstances" and until the last breath.*

It is easy to avoid responsibility for how life is to be lived in our day. Therefore, this insistence on the freedom of choice is a welcome one. (*S/R,* 44.)

For some, religion is an escape from freedom, an escape from accepting personal responsibility by submitting completely to an authoritarian God. Erich Fromm in *Escape From Freedom* writes about the tendency of modern man to run from the problems of freedom into some system of political totalitarianism. He is also talking, by implication, of the religious world. Much of the criticism made against religion by Sigmund Freud was directed against the kind of religion that gives up personal autonomy in the presence of an all-powerful, autocratic Father. (*S/R,* 45.)

Mature religion, however, is the expression of the man who recognizes his own worth and sees himself in a responsible partnership relationship with God. Like Job, he dares to "defend his ways" against God (Job 13:15). He is not so dependent on God that he must hold on to him in totally dependent ways. He dares to stand up to God. He trusts God to see him as one worthy of having his own ideas, willing to let him go his own way.

But knowing himself to be a unique and autonomous person, man is also free to let go, to put himself under God's authority, to accept God's leadership in his life. Just as the Prodigal Son was able to say to his father, "Make me as one of your servants," so the autonomous person can accept God's lordship over his life without feeling he has sacrificed his own unique individuality. (*S/R,* 46.)

■ Individually, scan again the portion of the text beginning with the words, "The degree to . . . ," on page 57 and ending with the words, "and win," on page 59.

Then, on the basis of this passage, underline the phrase that best expresses your understanding of your relationship to God:

Do Thou
Thou Shalt
Thou Mayest

Discuss together: How does your idea of God's authority affect your idea of persons in authority? How does your experience with

persons in authority affect your idea of God? At what points do you feel you need to grow in ability to accept God's leadership?
■ Close the session by praying together the "Prayer of Saint Francis" (Resource Packet, item 3).
■ Take the necessary assignments for through-the-week study or preparation.

NOTES ON CHAPTER 3

Page 48: Arthur Miller, *After the Fall* (Viking Press, 1964), page 46. Copyright © 1964 by Arthur Miller. Used by permission of the publisher.

Page 49: *After the Fall*, page 46. Used by permission.

Page 49: *After the Fall*, page 47. Used by permission.

Page 50: Sloan Wilson, *The Man in the Gray Flannel Suit* (Simon and Schuster, 1955), page 202. Used by permission.

Page 50: *The Man in the Gray Flannel Suit*, page 202. Used by permission.

Page 50: *The Man in the Gray Flannel Suit*, page 300. Used by permission.

Page 51: Carl Rogers, *On Becoming a Person* (Houghton Mifflin Company, 1961), page 16. Used by permission.

Page 51: Paul Tournier, *The Meaning of Persons* (Harper and Row, 1957), page 136. Copyright 1957 by Paul Tournier. Used by permission.

Page 54: Quoted by Richard Goldstein, "Drugs on the Campus," *The Saturday Evening Post*, June 4, 1966, page 42. Copyright © 1966 by the Curtis Publishing Company. Used by permission.

Page 58: John Steinbeck, *East of Eden* (Viking Press, 1952), page 268. Copyright 1952 by John Steinbeck. Used by permission of the publisher.

Page 58: *East of Eden*, page 270. Used by permission.

Page 59: *East of Eden*, page 303. Used by permission.

Page 59: Viktor E. Frankl, *Man's Search for Meaning* (Washington Square Press, 1963), page 214. Copyright 1959, 1962 by Viktor Frankl. Used by permission of Beacon Press.

Page 59: Viktor E. Frankl, *Homo Patiens*, translated by Donald Tweedie (Franz Deuticke, 1950), page 66.

2 Samuel 23:13-17
David's symbolic act of thanksgiving. (S/R, 47.)
1 Samuel 16:14-23
David's music refreshes Saul.
2 Samuel 6:16-22
David's dance of joy.
(*Read these selections in your Bible.*)

4
□□

WHAT'S IN THE MIRROR?

Walking from the parking lot to the office, Archibald thought about his work. On the whole, he was rather well satisfied. He knew his job thoroughly and performed it well enough to get periodic raises. But somehow it was not fulfilling. He never felt that his talents were being used to the full. The job just didn't challenge him. Or maybe he had lost the capacity to be challenged. He remembered the enthusiasm with which a friend had talked of the opportunities in the use of atomic power for peace. He wished he had something of that same enthusiasm. Or take that visitor from Russia. Communism must have something if it could call forth the kind of commitment the visitor had shown. Archibald just couldn't get excited about much of anything. Somehow he wasn't free to do much except follow the same old routine. And retirement was still a long way off. He often wondered what made him different from his friends who made so much more of their lives.

■ *As you arrive at your place of meeting, check the assignment chart for specific preparation to be made before the session begins.*

To adventure into the unknown calls for a freedom that some have never developed. Many feel that their capacities are not really being used. They have never learned to "launch out into the deep" (Luke 5:4), to risk the unknown. To adventure into new places is to invite uncertainty. When the poet Robert Frost tells of coming to a fork in a road and taking "the one less traveled by," * he is telling us the secret of his genius. Like most creative persons, he dares to take the initiative in going the less-traveled way. He is open to new experiences. He is free to allow his imagination to entertain unfamiliar thoughts. He doesn't need the security of the familiar, the usual, the routine pattern. He dares to stand alone because he dares to believe in his own judgment. (S/R, 48.)

A part of the appeal of the biblical David lies in his freedom to be different. He was a mighty warrior, yet skilled, too, in the harp. He could take on Goliath single-handed. He could also soothe King Saul's mood of depression. He could throw himself with abandon into a dance of joy and could argue against those who criticized his lack of dignity. He could see deep into life, could see meaning in ordinary events in a way that few others could. He was free to explore new ways of thinking. He had a keen sense of the presence of God in all of life, even though he sometimes chose to ignore God's ways. He could plot for his own pleasure and then could feel great remorse for his wrongdoing. He was free to achieve greatness and was free to acknowledge his sinfulness.

To be sure, freedom for its own sake is no particular virtue. Freedom without responsible direction leads to chaos. (S/R, 49.) The greatness of David lay in the fact that his free spirit was constantly called to account. He had a keen sense of God's claim on his life. The good he achieved came through responsible response to God. The evil that he pursued came when he used his freedom to further his own purposes rather than God's. The attainment of freedom is only half the task. But for many, the gaining of freedom comes with difficulty. David's life is instructive for understanding how freedom develops.

DEVELOPING INITIATIVE

When Archibald thought back over his boyhood, he could sense that limits had been placed early on his activities. For one thing, he had worn glasses as long as he could remember, so he had stayed out of fights. Moreover, in his home angry emotions had seldom been expressed. He could hardly recall ever having heard his father raise his voice in anger. Somehow it had been important to keep things peaceful and Archibald had readily adopted this same outlook. He recalled, for example, that in about the fourth grade a teacher had criticized a class for singing poorly, only to discover that her music book had a misprint so that it was different from the pupils' books. When she asked if anyone had noticed the difference, Archibald had admitted that he had. He recalled how she said to him: "Archibald, you could make so much more of yourself if you would only speak up more." But he seldom did. And now the pattern was deep-set.

In contrast to Archibald, David's early life had been one that encouraged the development of his abilities. As a shepherd, he had learned to protect his sheep against wild animals. He did not hesitate to stand up to his brothers. His father trusted him to carry messages far from home. He was known as one "skilful in playing [the harp], a man of valor, a man of war" (1 Samuel 16:18). He was equally at home in music and in warfare. His natural abilities were developed in an atmosphere of freedom.

One goal in childhood is to develop a freedom to take the initiative. Patterns of conformity or of taking the initiative are started quite early in life. They often remain fixed for most of life. The years just before the child goes to school are the years when initiative is encouraged or discouraged. Many adults continue in adult life to express the patterns developed in childhood. One author, W. Hugh Missildine, has a book entitled *Your Inner Child of the Past*. In this book

65

Missildine suggests that most of the problems of adult life are due to inappropriate patterns established in childhood. Missildine says that many attitudes were developed in childhood in the attempt to cope with parents. Even though in adult life the parent is no longer a threat, the attitudes developed early tend to persist. (S/R, 50.)

With the best of intentions, parents often stifle efforts at initiative. The preschool child is filled with curiosity about life around him. In the natural course of events he begins to explore in all directions. The parent, fearful that the child will get hurt, tends to surround him with prohibitions: Don't climb the tree, you might fall down. Don't get out of sight, you might get lost. Natural curiosity that can flower into creative and imaginative living is easily discouraged so that life becomes routine and dull. (S/R, 51.)

On the other hand, some parents will encourage curiosity, no matter how it is expressed. Here are the parents who take time to answer the child's questions, who deal freely with curiosity in all areas, including sex. Such parents go to considerable pains to confront the child with new experiences. Through travel, camping, reading, and selected TV programs, the child's world is expanded. Teachers join here with parents to encourage curiosity and to stimulate imagination.

David was free to express his feelings in dramatic acts. His wife, Michal, criticized him for dancing without embarrassment before the people (2 Samuel 6:20-22). Michal thought that it was beneath the dignity of the king to display himself before the servants. David refused to acknowledge any inappropriateness, declaring that the people would understand his exuberance and the joy with which he was expressing his relationship to God. (S/R, 52.) He was an individualist who would not be bound by custom. He was free to allow his feelings to emerge in dance.

The freedom to be different, to be independent in judgment, to take the initiative in doing things in unusual ways is a distinguishing mark of the most creative person. Creativity, however, does not necessarily result from freedom. It is when freedom is combined with responsible commitment to meaningful goals that genuine creativity emerges. The struggle to keep growing toward significant objectives without giving in to the tendency to settle back into familiar ruts is a problem for most of us. It takes constant effort to grow in new and untried ways. As we will see later, the issue becomes particularly acute in middle age. (S/R, 53.) In A. J. Cronin's novel *The Citadel*, the young wife cries out passionately to her disillusioned husband, who as a young doctor has given up his early idealism in order to make money:

> "Don't make a joke of it, darling. You usen't to talk that way. Oh! Don't you see, don't you see, you're falling a victim to the very system you used to run down, the thing you used to hate?" Her face was pitiful in its agitation. "Don't you remember how you used to speak of life, that it was an attack on the unknown, an assault uphill—as though you had to take some castle that you knew was there, but couldn't see, on the top—"
> He muttered uncomfortably:—
> "Oh! I was young then—foolish. That was just romantic talk. . . ." *

He had stopped taking the initiative, had stopped growing, had settled back into comfortable, unimaginative ways. He had lost the sense of obligation.

The young doctor in Cronin's novel illustrates the tension between an ordered, structured routine and a creative approach that disturbs the customary pattern. Much of the ministry of Jesus was directed toward breaking up patterns that were stifling growth. He was constantly challenging people to break out of routines that left them uninspired and to risk a new way of adventure. He knew that to keep growing requires a willingness to give up the customary patterns momentarily. Safety and security must be given up for the moment in order that progress can be made toward a new goal. It is like striking out without a clear destination in mind, but with a compass reading to follow.

Jesus insisted that the sense of direction was all important but that the specific pathway might take many forms. He was very clear about living a life in accord with God's will, but he never tried to spell out every detail of what this life would be. Indeed, much of his protest was against life lived under the stipulations of the rigid Jewish law.

Creative people are often unorthodox. The freedom that they feel to forsake the usual patterns makes it possible for them to explore new and untried ways, even though these explorations often bring criticism from the culture. Research with the *most* creative persons, however, suggests that true creativity is found in persons who are very responsible in their approach to life. They look more like the picture of the business executive who carries work home in his briefcase than like the bearded and sandaled beatnik. (*S/R,* 54.)

■ Set goals for your study of this chapter as suggested on pages 15-16.
■ Listen to a dialogue entitled "I Dare You" (Resource Packet, item 6) . You will need *two* characters: a man who pretends to be driving to work and one person to be the voice. See the Leaders' Guide for further directions.
■ In groups of two to four persons discuss: What reasons for not responding do you, personally, give to the inner voice urging you to exercise freedom?
　Read silently *S/R,* 53. How can we continue to grow in new and untried ways rather than give in to the tendency to settle into familiar ruts? How can you be free to be different and to express independent judgment? Let one member of your small group read aloud, but quietly, *S/R,* 48. Share an experience in which you dared to take the initiative and go the less traveled way.

REMOVING UNREALISTIC GUILT

As Archibald approached the business section of the city, he passed a police car parked at the curb. He felt his muscles tighten and sensed a tenseness in his whole body. It was ridiculous, of course, because he wasn't doing anything wrong and the officer wasn't even interested in him. Nevertheless, the reaction was there. Archibald never felt comfortable in the presence of the law. Indeed, the feeling wasn't limited to policemen. Anyone in authority, including his boss, seemed to bring out the worst in him. Imogene often told Archibald that he seemed like a different person when his boss was around. It was almost as if he couldn't think straight, couldn't think for himself, with his boss there. Somehow he seemed to be less of a man in the presence of someone in authority.

The feeling of anxiety that Archibald recognizes is a common result of trying to become independent. One of the ways in which a child learns to see himself as an individual is by seeing himself in relationship to others. Sometimes this means competition with others, and competition easily leads to feelings of guilt. If a person feels guilty, his initiative is stifled. The familiar parable of the talents is a good illustration of how anxiety hinders initiative. The servant who had received only one piece of money had hidden it in the ground because, as he said, "I was afraid" (Matthew 25:25). His fear prevented him from taking the initiative to put his money to work.

Conflict between father and son or mother and daughter is a common problem in life. David, the king, knew this problem in his own household. His son, Absalom, plotted against him, overthrew him, and usurped the throne (2 Samuel 15:1-12). David regained the throne, but his son was killed in the process. The struggle between David and Absalom was the natural outgrowth of a situation where an overprivileged son struggled to discover who he was apart from his father who was the king. To some degree, conflict in the home between the generations, and especially between members of the same sex, cannot be avoided. A child sees himself as an individual by separating himself from too close a resemblance to his parents. (S/R, 55.)

In John Steinbeck's *East of Eden* the struggle of Caleb, the son, with Adam, the father, is one of the central themes. Caleb seems to do everything wrong. Trying desperately to please his father, he succeeds only in arousing his anger. Adam's ambitious plans to send refrigerated lettuce to Chicago from California fails miserably and he loses many thousands of dollars. Caleb sets to work to make up the loss. He enters into partnership with a businessman who foresees war coming and makes a large profit over wheat bought in ad-

69

vance. Caleb then presents his father with cash to make up for the loss in the lettuce fiasco. But to Caleb's dismay his father not only rejects the money but criticizes the son unmercifully for exploiting farmers in wartime. It is his father's rejection of his efforts and the father's apparent lack of love for him that leads Caleb to destroy his brother, Aron. To his father who is on his deathbed, Caleb cries:

> "I'm sorry, Father."
> ". . . I did it. . . . I'm responsible for Aron's death and for your sickness. . . . I don't want to do bad things—but I do them." *

The long-time servant Lee pleads with the father.

> ". . . Here is your son—Caleb—your only son. Look at him, Adam!"
>
> .   .   .   .
>
> "He did a thing in anger, Adam, because he thought you had rejected him. The result of his anger is that his brother and your son is dead."
>
> .   .   .   .
>
> ". . . Your son is marked with guilt out of himself—out of himself—almost more than he can bear. Don't crush him with rejection. Don't crush him, Adam."
> "Adam, give him your blessing." *

There can be little direction or purpose in life without the freedom that releases a person from the bonds of guilt. Caleb Trask is freed from his guilt by Adam's blessing, and the future is then open for him. His father's love was necessary to offset the rejection that he had felt. Until Caleb sensed that the relationship with his father was right, he was bound by guilt that he could not free himself from. Lee put the issue very clearly to Adam: ". . . Give him his chance. Let him be free. That's all a man has over the beasts. Free him! Bless him!" *

It is the Christian affirmation that God does give the blessing, that God does free man from his guilt. (S/R, 56.) The father in the Prodigal Son story goes out to meet his son with the promise of a feast to celebrate his return. It is obvious that the father represents the accepting, forgiving

Father-God. The New Testament teaches that God accepts man while he is still a sinner. Man is acceptable to God, not because of his righteous deeds but as though he were righteous, if he truly puts his trust in God and is penitent because of his sin and unbelief. Regardless of what we have done, if we repent, God "is faithful and just, and will forgive our sins and cleanse us from all unrighteousness" (1 John 1:9). (S/R, 57.)

It is obvious that much behavior in children is not approved by parents. Such behavior, however, is not to be understood as typical of what the child wants to do but as the expression of a frustration too great for him to handle. No child wants to be cut off from his parents. When his behavior results in a momentary barrier between him and his parents, he is in distress. Because he is young and inexperienced, he needs help in finding his way back into favor. Whereas most children resist being forced into any pattern of behavior, they respond readily to suggestions about doing something else. The son who won't stop teasing his sister will turn from her quickly when his father offers to play checkers with him.

Most children handle their relationships with their parents by becoming like the parents, by identifying with them. The little boy can then dare to handle life in the pattern of his father, and the little girl handles life in the pattern of her mother. Being like the parent, the child feels no threat from the parent. Rather than feeling guilty about his behavior, he feels proud to be acting "like daddy." (S/R, 58.) Free from guilt feelings, he is more able to take the initiative, to respond to challenge, to strive toward worthwhile goals. (S/R, 59 and 60.)

■ Read in unison the Prayer of Humble Access (S/R, 59). How do you feel as you pray this prayer? In what sense, if any, do you feel unworthy? Let individuals describe their feelings aloud. Then one person may read aloud, while others follow the text silently, S/R, 60.

Discuss in the total group: What is theological guilt? How would you distinguish it from other feelings of guilt? When might theological guilt become neurotic guilt? How may one experience release from theological guilt? Do you, as individuals, feel a sense of guilt for crimes of war and injustice? Should you? Why might individuals feel no sense of guilt for sin?

■ Divide the class into three groups for study.

Group A will study the story of Absalom and David (2 Samuel 13:30-39; 14:21-23; 15:1-17; 17:1-15; 18:1-14, 19-33.)

Group B will study the story of Caleb and Adam from *East of Eden*, beginning with the words, "Conflict between . . ." on page 69 and ending with the words, "Bless him!" on page 70.

Group C will study the story of the Prodigal Son and his father (Luke 15:11-24).

Each group should also read *S/R,* 55.

Consider some of these questions: What factors were at work causing feelings of guilt? limiting freedom? How does guilt stifle purpose and direction? What did the father do to cause the conflict? Where and how is freedom achieved? Compare the father's action with our understanding of God's acceptance of us. How does the father's action compare with God's action in helping us to be free? How does God help us to be free?

DEVELOPING CONSCIENCE

Whenever Archibald's thoughts turned to his boss, he became uncomfortable. It was as if he suddenly became a little boy in short pants. He became tongue-tied and embarrassed. He knew that his boss was a nice guy and an understanding person, but nevertheless his anxiety always mounted in the boss's presence. Imogene had never been able to understand this reaction. She treated his boss just as she treated everyone else, in a very natural, comfortable way. And the boss seemed to like it! Archibald knew that this was an area in which he needed to grow. After all, there would always be a boss around.

One of the strongest forces preventing growth toward maturity is a conscience that hasn't grown up. In his novel *Arundel,* Kenneth Roberts gives a good illustration of how attitudes that are formed in childhood and never revised can be self-defeating. Young Steven Nason falls violently in love with Mary Mollinson when they are children. He asserts his love for her and declares that he will marry her. Having promised his love to her, he feels obliged to remain true to her over the years. He ignores every other girl. His blind love is based on the emotion of a child and is never evaluated in terms of adult standards. When some years later he is scouting for the American army, he discovers Mary living in Quebec as the mistress of a British officer. She isn't anything like the idealized image that he has carried with him for so long. Only then is he able to see how foolish he has been to remain loyal to a childish promise. Steven is not able to escape from bondage to his youthful promise until he sees Mary as the army follower.

Many of us never fulfill our potential because of attitudes developed early in life and never revised. To learn that "anything worth doing is worth doing well" is fine for the growing child who needs to learn to commit himself to a task. But to make this saying a cardinal rule for life is ridiculous. Children are often taught to clean their plates in the interest of good health through a balanced diet. To go through life always eating every scrap left on a plate is to become a slave to a childish habit. To be taught to "finish what you start" is a good rule for a child in developing discipline, but to make this a rule for the adult is to overlook the power of critical evaluation. Some books aren't worth finishing, and some tasks are better left undone. *Ideas ought to change as a part of the growing process, or direction for life is limited to childlike goals. (S/R, 61.)*

Rabbi Joshua Loth Liebman in his book, *Peace of Mind,* gives a descriptive title to one of his chapters: "Conscience Doth Make Cowards." Many rules about right and wrong, when first established in childhood, tend to become rigid standards for all of life when, actually, they are appropriate only for the years of childhood. *Much of the ministry of Jesus was directed toward a life lived not by law but by spirit.* Much of the writing of Paul tries to work out this distinction. Of course, it is a good thing to "remember the sabbath day, to keep it holy" (Exodus 20:8), but Jesus insisted, "The sabbath was made for man, not man for the sabbath" (Mark 2:27). Life would be simpler if it could be lived by law. Indeed, some try to live that way, but life is not like law. Life is always changing, always growing. The rules by which it is lived need to be growing, too.

The problem of the rich young ruler (Mark 10:17-22), as we have already seen, was that his life in adult years was still directed by the rigid rules of the law. Laws are needed to provide a structure for life, but laws in themselves are never adequate for giving direction to life. The transition from life lived according to external rules to life directed by an inner spirit is a major one and marks the real difference between childhood and adulthood. The one thing the rich young ruler lacked was a sense of direction from within. He was seeking to find in law that which can only come from an inner attitude. No wonder his life had lost any real sense of meaning.

We have learned about conscience through the writings of depth psychology. Freud uses the term *superego* to describe the standards of right and wrong that are implanted in a person's life by his culture and largely by his parents. In its early stages the superego and the conscience can be related. A person discovers what is right and what is wrong, not in some magical way as if implanted by God but through the normal channels of learning to be human in a society of people. (*S/R*, 62.) Freud failed to see, however, that the conscience can grow up. For Freud, the superego was formed in the preschool years and never really changed. The superego is like the archaic conscience, like the childish conscience that hasn't grown up.

To be sure, in all too many lives the conscience remains in the superego state: immature, undeveloped, dictatorial, arbitrary. Such a conscience can cause all kinds of trouble, can create all kinds of guilt, can thwart most forward movement. Sometimes it takes psychotherapy to discover how inappropriate many attitudes are and how foolish it is not to recognize negative feelings. To come to terms with reality is to recognize that we do have lustful and envious and resentful and angry feelings! (*S/R*, 63.) These need not be denied; they cannot be brought under control until they are identified and acknowledged. *Much initiative is stifled by unre-solved negative emotions that create feelings of guilt, tie up energy, and lead to feelings of inadequacy.*

■ Examine your conscience. Check yes or no.
I am more interested in what I should do than why I should do it.
————yes ————no
I feel that whatever is legal is moral. ————yes ————no
I feel guilty when I show hostile feelings. ————yes ————no
    Analyze your answers by checking them against the italicized statements on pages 72-75. Read silently *S/R,* 62 and 63.
    Discuss in the total group: How do you feel about the italicized statements? What is your reaction to the Selected Readings? How can we identify and acknowledge negative feelings toward ourselves and others? Is it easier to live by the law or by the spirit? Why? How can we gain freedom from standards and rules established in child-hood that are inappropriate in adult life? How has your idea of God and your relationship to him grown and changed over the years?

FINDING DIRECTION IN FAITH

Archibald sensed that the attitudes he held toward his boss were like the attitudes he held toward God. But there was a difference, too. His religious life played a part in everything he did, whereas his boss was important to him only on the job. From his boss he received specific directions about how to carry on business, but from his faith he received a sense of direction about where he was going. The specific instruc-tions from his boss, however, were usually much clearer than the sense of direction about his life.

Our faith asserts that life can be given direction. The faith is expressed in Job in these words: "Why is light given to man whose way is hid,/whom God has hedged in?" (Job 3:23). Light *is* given, a path *can* be found even though a direct route is blocked. There *is* a way out, even though hedges seem to block is off. A freedom to find the way out is sometimes blocked.

Helen Keller's release from a world of darkness and silence is the heart-warming story of a teacher who gave direction to a little child's life. The story is told by William Gibson in his play *The Miracle Worker.* This play was made into a popular movie. Helen Keller was a blind, deaf-mute child, cut off from all real communication with life. She was taken in hand by a young teacher, Annie Sullivan, who had grown up in a mental hospital and had only recently recovered from blindness.

Annie Sullivan knew that to help little Helen to find direction for her life there had to be some meaning in her existence. It wasn't enough to behave; she needed to be able to communicate, too. Annie saw in Helen the potential person that was waiting to be called forth.

Then the breakthrough came. Helen suddenly made the connection between letters spelled in her hand and the objects the letters stood for. Now she could communicate. Now she could make sense out of things. Now she could find purpose for her life. But first the darkness and the silence had to be penetrated.

Direction and purpose in life come only when initiative is stronger than guilt. But guilt over our own inadequacies need not bind us forever. The late theologian Paul Tillich reminds us that the heart of the Christian method lies in God's acceptance of us even though we are unacceptable. He talks of "the courage to be" as the courage to accept one's self even in his unacceptability. (Turn back and read again S/R, 34 in Chapter 3.) We stand before God, not according to what we deserve, but according to what we are. God does not condemn us for our failure to live up to the last letter of the law. (S/R, 64.) He accepts us with the full recognition of our human failings. Paul's testimony is very genuine. As long as he tried to find favor in God's sight by living according to God's law, he was wretched. "Wretched man that I am! Who will deliver me from this body of death?" (Romans 7:24.) He provides his own answer, the answer that looks beyond the law to the spirit: "Thanks be to God through Jesus Christ our Lord!" (Romans 7:25.)

■ Listen as a member of the group reads aloud S/R, 34. What kind of responsibility do you have in accepting your acceptance by God?
■ Share, spontaneously, any insights you have gained from reading

this chapter or from class activities. How have your ideas changed? Read aloud or paraphrase particular statements to which you wish to react.

■ Pray together the "Prayer of Saint Francis" (Resource Packet, item 3).

■ One person should be selected now to be prepared to report an interview with a medical doctor or psychiatrist as suggested in the procedures on pages 97-98.

■ Take the necessary assignments for through-the-week study.

NOTES ON CHAPTER 4

Page 64: Robert Frost, "The Road Not Taken," *Complete Poems of Robert Frost* (Holt, Rinehart and Winston, 1949), page 131. Copyright 1916 by Holt, Rinehart and Winston. Copyright 1944 by Robert Frost. Used by permission.

Page 67: A. J. Cronin, *The Citadel* (Little, Brown and Company, 1937), pages 299-300. Copyright 1937 by A. J. Cronin. Used by permission of the publisher.

Page 70: John Steinbeck, *East of Eden* (Viking Press, 1952), page 595. Copyright 1952 by John Steinbeck. Used by permission of the publisher.

Page 70: *East of Eden*, page 602. Used by permission.

Page 70: *East of Eden*, page 602. Used by permission.

Matthew 16:13-23
Simon is named Peter. (*S/R,* 65.)

Luke 5:1-11
Jesus meets Peter.

Mark 14:25-72
Peter denies Jesus.

John 21:15-17
Jesus challenges Peter.

(Read these selections in your Bible.)

5

□□
WE'RE FREE, WE'RE FREE!

As he entered the office, Archibald's mood changed. He felt good to be there in such a familiar setting. Years of training and experience helped him to feel able to handle most anything that might come up. He liked the feeling of satisfaction over work completed. He enjoyed his contacts with his fellow workers. He liked the sense of being involved with life that his work brought him. Even if his own life wasn't very exciting, he found satisfaction in watching the plans prepared in his office put into action. He knew that his work was important for him and he was glad to be busy. He knew he would be miserable without a demanding job to do, even though he often complained of the load of work placed upon him.

Most of us need a job to perform. In our culture a sense of worth tends to be tied to having a job. To know that people count on us for getting the work done is a strong reason

■ *As you arrive at your place of meeting, check the assignment chart for specific preparation to be made before the session begins.*

for staying on the job, even when we feel like quitting. Most of us at any age see ourselves as important in terms of the work that we accomplish. To be a failure at work is hard to take. To be involved in a worthwhile task is to find meaning in life. (*S/R*, 66.)

One of the best examples of a man who was transformed by a meaningful task is Simon Peter. A clear picture of Peter emerges from the gospel record. He was a man of quick and changing emotions, a husky fisherman with a great love of life. He is best known as the disciple who denied his Lord in the time of testing, yet he became one of the leaders of the early Christian church. He not only carried the word about Jesus far and wide within the Jewish world, but he took it into the Gentile world as well. Tradition has it that he died a martyr's death in Rome. Who would have guessed that unstable, bungling Simon could become Peter, the solid rock who would die the martyr's death?

DEVELOPING A FEELING OF COMPETENCE

Archibald was not one to talk a lot. Imogene often complained that he seldom told her anything until she asked about it. He knew that talking wasn't easy for him.

Talking about his work was even more difficult. He could never quite put into words what his job meant to him. In a way hard to describe it made him feel worthwhile. It provided a center around which almost everything else revolved. It put him in touch with life. It gave him a chance to influence the lives of others. It gave him a sense of personal importance. It helped him to feel that he was competent to handle life.

Not everyone feels competent. Some years ago I led a class in a clinic dealing with emotional problems. One of the clinic members began calling the class the "Can Do Class." It was an apt description for what he had learned. He had learned that he could do a lot more for himself than he had realized. His help actually came most directly when he tried to help others. Accepting as a task the aiding of others in the class, he made significant progress himself.

Peter was very much in this situation. His strength became apparent not while he was a fisherman but when he became Christ's loyal lieutenant, a fisher of men. The picture given of Peter in the Book of Acts is far different from the inept, ineffective although lovable man revealed in the Gospels. One recorded sentence tells volumes: "Now when they saw the boldness of Peter and John . . . they recognized that they had been with Jesus" (Acts 4:13). Peter's competence emerged after Pentecost when he was given a task to do. He literally changed from ineffective Simon to competent Peter (the rock).

Some of the deepest roots to the feeling of competence are found in the early school years. When the child is about eight years of age, he can begin to handle his more sensitive muscles to bring them under control. The boy learns to bat the ball. The girl learns to sew her doll's clothes. For the first time the child begins to think about life in adult-like terms. He realizes that authority has to be obeyed, that pleasure sometimes has to be postponed, that death comes eventually to everyone. It is in these years that his picture of himself as a going concern in the world can emerge. He can learn to see himself as an effective member of society. (S/R, 67.)

The importance of the peer group—that is, a group of about the same age and status—for developing a feeling of competence cannot be overstressed. Indeed, many parents who feel unequal to the task of parenthood take comfort in the knowledge that their training is reinforced by what their children learn in play with other children. Boys and girls learn a good deal about life as they play together on a playground, especially as they play games with no adults around. It doesn't take a boy long to realize that if he wants to get his turn at bat in a baseball game, some kind of rules have to be introduced. He becomes willing to have only three strikes at bat because he discovers that this is the only way everyone, including himself, can get his turn in batting. He discovers, too, that playing ball is a team sport where, instead of going for a home run each time at bat, he may be asked to lay down a sacrifice bunt. The sacrifice is just what the word implies: he risks being put out in order to allow his teammate to advance. He also learns that a sacrifice does not count against his batting record. When the record is averaged, a sacrifice is not counted as a time at bat. There is no penalty for helping the team.

There is still another task in the early school years. In addition to the task of accommodation to the social scene, there is also the task of coming to terms with persons in authority. (*S/R,* 68.) As many new authority figures are introduced, the child has a chance to re-evaluate his attitude toward the authority of his parents. Other adults now share the authority role, and suddenly the child is asked to conform to new standards. The child who rules his parents' home like a petty tyrant discovers that the world isn't like his home. The modest and docile child discovers that he can be more aggressive without being destroyed. These early school years are a time for remedying the limitations of the home, a time for really learning to be a social being.

■ Set goals for your study of this chapter as suggested on pages 15-16.
■ In groups of four persons, recall if there were experiences in childhood in which you learned to see yourself as competent. Were these experiences in the academic, or economic, or social, or athletic areas? Do you see a relationship between your current attitudes toward your competence and your childhood experiences? In what specific ways have your ideas of competence been modified as a result of exposure to hero figures and models of competence such as teachers, coaches, scout leaders, and successful businessmen? What are the problems faced by the child or young person learning to see himself as an effective member of society and coming to terms with persons in authority? See *S/R,* 67 and 68. What should be the attitude and responsibility of the adult?

Share significant insights and conclusions with the entire group.

SETTING ASIDE FEARS OF FAILURE

Archibald had learned in his peer group to deal with failure. In a training program intended to develop greater sensitivity to the needs of others, Archibald had realized that failure was not the worst thing that could happen. He had expressed his discovery in a simple sentence: "I can dare to fail." He no longer had to succeed in everything he attempted. Unafraid of failure, he was then free to attempt many new experiences, confident that he could work things out whether he was successful or not. With this simple affirmation, life was suddenly opened up for him. He had learned, as Peter had, that failure need not be the last word.

It is not by chance that Arthur Miller's play *Death of a Salesman* received favorable response when it first appeared in 1949, or that its TV revival in 1966 won acclaim as one of the best shows of the year. The movie version of the play continues to be shown to responsive audiences. It is the story of a small-time shoe salesman, Willy Loman, whose love of his family, his house, his garden, and all the little things in life is sacrificed because of his need to be a success. He is not content to be a loving father, a faithful husband, a happy gardener. He must also be a great success with the merchants of Boston, Waterbury, Portland, and Bangor, even if it means becoming deceptive as a businessman and unfaithful as a husband. His need to be a success blinds him to little acts of dishonesty that prove eventually to be his undoing. Willy never was very good at seeing life as it was. Even as he considers suicide and the funeral that would follow, he looks through the eyes of fantasy. Speaking to his Uncle Ben about his son, Willy says:

> ". . . He thinks I'm nothing, see, and so he spites me. But the funeral—*Straightening up:* Ben, that funeral will be massive! They'll come. from Maine, Massachusetts, Vermont, New Hampshire! All the old-timers with the strange license plates—that boy will be thunder-struck, Ben, because he never realized— I am known! Rhode Island, New York, New Jersey—I am known, Ben, and he'll see it with his eyes once and for all. He'll see what I am, Ben! He's in for a shock, that boy!" *

When the suicide does take place, no one comes to the funeral. In the closing scene of the play, Arthur Miller has written some lines that have led many people to rethink the American emphasis on success. Willy's wife, Linda, is talking with Willy's brother, Charley, and with her son, Biff:

Linda.	"Why didn't anybody come?"
Charley.	"It was a very nice funeral."
Linda.	"But where were all the people he knew? Maybe they blame him."
Charley.	"Naa. It's a rough world, Linda. They wouldn't blame him."
Linda.	"I can't understand it. All this time especially. First time in thirty-five years we were just about free and clear. He only needed a little salary. He was even finished with the dentist."
Charley.	"No man only needs a little salary."
Linda.	"I can't understand it."
Biff.	"There were a lot of nice days. When he'd come home from a trip; or on Sundays, making the stoop; finishing the cellar; putting on the new porch; when he built the extra bathroom; and put up the garage. You know something, Charley, there's more of him in that front stoop than in all the sales he ever made."
Charley.	"Yeah. He was a happy man with a batch of cement."
Linda.	"He was so wonderful with his hands."
Biff.	"He had the wrong dreams. All, all, wrong."

. . . .

Biff.	"Charley, the man didn't know who he was."

. . . .

Biff.	"Let's go, Mom."
Linda.	"I'll be with you in a minute. Go on, Charley . . . I want to, just for a minute. I never had a chance to say good-by."
Linda.	"Forgive me, dear. I can't cry. I don't know what it is, but I can't cry. I don't understand it. Why did you ever do that? Help me, Willy, I can't cry. It seems to me that you're just on another trip. I keep expecting you. Willy, dear, I can't cry. Why did you do it? I search and search and I search, and I can't understand it, Willy. I made the last payment on the house today. Today, dear. And there'll be nobody home . . . We're free and clear . . . We're free . . . We're free . . . We're free." *

The tragedy in Linda's final words is very real. The freedom she and Willy had sought for so long finally came when it was too late to be enjoyed.

When Biff spoke of his father's wrong dreams, he was referring to Willy's life orientation. The real tragedy was that Willy sought success in terms of personal recognition. His real need was to develop his own unique potential. In his need to achieve, Willy had no sense of a claim of God upon his life. (*S/R*, 69.) He saw himself victimized by his culture rather than in any sense in control of it. Biff was right when he said that Willy "didn't know who he was."

Simon Peter didn't know who he was, either, but he was helped to become the man that was potentially present all the time. Peter found himself as he found something great enough to give himself to. The impact of the gospel has always had such force on the lives of those who have really opened themselves to it.

■ In the same groups of four persons, read from your Bibles the four references to Peter mentioned at the beginning of this chapter.
  Then, with each member of your group taking a part (a narrator and three characters), read quietly the excerpt from *Death of a Salesman* (page 84).
  Discuss together: What ideas do you get about competence and failure from the stories of Peter and Willy? What, in each case, contributed to a sense of competence or a sense of failure? How do you define success? Consider *S/R*, 85. How could the need to succeed cause us to lose track of who we are? What difference is made by a sense of God's claim on our lives?
  ■ See the movie, *Death of a Salesman*. Perhaps you could request your local theater to schedule the showing of the movie as a part of its regular programing. This would need to be planned well in advance of this lesson. The film is also available for rental. Film catalogues would list the source and the rental fee. Have alternate dates in mind in case it is not available on your preferred date. Follow the viewing of the film with class discussion.
  Or you may wish to listen to the recording of *Death of a Salesman* featuring Thomas Mitchell (Decca, DX-102). The class might purchase the recording and place it in the church library after use, or perhaps you could borrow it from an individual or the public library.

ACHIEVEMENT IN SERVICE

For Archibald, his faith had always been a quiet sort of thing. When his neighbors who were scientists teased him about holding to old-fashioned ideas about religion, he never knew how to answer them. (S/R, 70.) He had many ·questions about belief, but he was very certain about one thing. Through his church, he found a way to relate himself to some of the greatest personalities that the world had ever known. Every time he placed his offering in the collection plate he felt a part of the world-wide activity of his church. He couldn't serve in some distant outpost himself, but he could share in the work through his giving. Without ever leaving home, he had a part in the work of men and women who had found special fields of service.

When Albert Schweitzer died on September 4, 1965, at the age of 96, the world was reminded again of the tremendous impact that one man had made upon the world. If ever there was a person whose life demonstrated what the power of Christian goals could do, it was Schweitzer. "I went to Africa," he wrote to a friend, "in obedience to Jesus." In contrast to Willy Loman, Schweitzer's entire life was lived by the highest principles. He achieved distinction in three major areas of life—theology, music, and medicine. In each of these fields he was first of all a follower of Jesus. (S/R, 71.) For him, Christianity was a channel through which his achievements found expression.

The story of Albert Schweitzer is well known. He had promising careers ahead of him either as a scholar of the Bible or as a concert organist. Instead, Schweitzer chose to enroll in medical school with the intent of going to the heart of Africa as a doctor. He simply wasn't able to enjoy a happy life while so many people were suffering with sickness and pain. The hospital village that he established at Lambaréné in French Equatorial Africa became the inspiration for at least half a dozen other similar institutions in remote, poverty-stricken areas. The greatest contribution that Schweitzer made to life was the inspiration that he provided for others.

We have already spoken of the explosive power of the Christian faith when it really seizes a person's life. The story of William Larimer Mellon, Jr., is the story of a rich man's son who was blasted out of a life of the idle rich into a life of dedicated service through reading about Albert Schweitzer. Mellon was thirty-seven at the time. He returned to college to complete undergraduate preparation, went on to medical school with fellow students about the age his sons could have been. When he received his M.D. at forty-four, he and his wife, Gwen, founded the Albert Schweitzer Hospital in Haiti, going to a people with a high disease rate and a low literacy rate almost within the shadow of prosperous, educated United States. And so the transforming power of Christianity continues to be a life-bringing force for good.

There is no question: persons like Albert Schweitzer and Larimer and Gwen Mellon have found deep meaning for their lives. Indeed, the unique contribution of each of these persons lies in his discovery that meaning in life is not dependent upon circumstances. Rather, it depends on the kind of response that one gives to circumstances. (*S/R*, 72.) Most of us are not likely to give witness to our faith in such dramatic ways as these persons have done, but each of us can live a life of service in his own place. The place in which service is given is not important but the fact that service is central is important. It may be volunteer service in a local hospital. It may be transportation service for those unable to move freely. It may be voter registration for those unacquainted with political procedures. It may be study help for slow learners. Wherever the opportunity for service is used to good advantage, a sense of achievement results. To be of use provides a strong support to a feeling of achievement. To be of service is to stand solidly in the tradition of Jesus of Nazareth. (*S/R*, 73.)

■ Display picture-chart "Self-Giving" (Resource Packet, item 7). A Leaders' Guide accompanies it. While the group looks at the pictures, one person may read Matthew 10:39. Pause for a moment of quiet meditation. A second person, who has prepared ahead of time, will then read *S/R*, 71.

Discuss in the group: According to the poem, where is Christ found? Is this where you expect to find Christ? In what sense can we free Christ?

Read silently *S/R, 73*. Then discuss together: How would you distinguish conventional charity from Christian service and witness? What are proper motives for Christian service? Cite examples of the ways we tyrannize persons we help. How can we avoid the temptation?

Study the pictures carefully. Do you agree that they portray genuine *self*-giving? Why? How are you expressing your faith in service?

THE NEED TO BE CHALLENGED

Archibald and Imogene often talked together about how they could help their children most. They knew that loving them meant more than smoothing the way for them. Archibald could recall a number of points in his life when the movement forward had been accomplished because of pressure placed upon him. He knew that the incentive of the Boy Scout program had helped him to go farther than he was inclined to go naturally. He remembered how competition in the high school track team had helped him to put forth the extra spurt that was needed to win the race. But it was hard to know when the challenge needed to be put and how to put it.

The hardest part of a counselor's task lies in timing. To know when to support and when to challenge, when to protect and when to nudge, calls for the greatest of skill. Jesus was a master at timing. With Peter he was constantly providing both support and challenge, with challenge the stronger note. When Jesus said to Peter, "Put out into the deep," he was talking about more than catching fish. It took Jesus to challenge him into effective achievement. (*S/R, 74.*)

The counselor's use of challenge is shown in the account of the recovery of Lisa and David. Dr. White has a talk with David about David's power to choose. The conversation began when David told the doctor it was his birthday.

David.	"I'm sixteen today."
Dr. White.	"Oh! Happy birthday."
David.	"About that talk we had—"
Dr. White.	"Which?"

David.	"You know, some time ago. Controlling time."
Dr. White.	"Oh yes. What about it?"
David.	"This business of choice. If you have a choice over the time, you said."
Dr. White.	"What about it?"
David.	(A look of disgust came over his face.) "Stop this pedantic what-about-it stuff! I'm asking you about it. It's your production, so can you spare a few words to elaborate on it?"
Dr. White.	"Choice means just that—choice. When people are not well, much of what they do is done because they have to do it. But if they get better and become themselves, then they are free to do as they please; they have a choice." *

David got the idea. Getting well was not something the doctor could do for him. He had to make a choice for health himself, but the doctor's carefully worded challenge helped.

Isabel Smith in her autobiography *Wish I Might* tells of how her physician, Dr. Trudeau, would combine challenge with support. Her discouragement in her bout with tuberculosis had taken most of the life out of her. Her doctor would speak sharply to her to rouse her out of her apathy. "My land, Izzy, what's the matter? Lying there as though the end of the world had come." Then he would offer his support: "Are you sunk, girl? Come on now, tell me all about it." * By refusing to treat her like an invalid, he challenged her to become the healthy person that she eventually became.

The challenge to achieve what we are capable of comes better in example than it does in words. The power of the example of one person to give heart to a whole group and to challenge them to bring out their best is portrayed in Anna Segher's novel *The Seventh Cross*. This is the story of George Heisler who, along with six other prisoners, escaped from Westhofen Concentration Camp. The commandant of the camp erected seven great crosses in the courtyard on which to hang the bodies of the prisoners when they were recaptured. Six of the crosses were filled, one by one, but the seventh remained empty. George Heisler remained at large.

Heisler was helped in his escape at one point by Dr. and Mrs. Kress. They risked their lives for him, but found something of the meaning of life restored to them in turn. After they had driven Heisler to his next contact, they sat together drinking coffee.

> . . . At last Frau Kress broke the silence that had lasted almost an hour. "Did he say anything at the end?"
> "No. Only 'Thanks!' "
> "It's strange," she said, "but I feel as if I should thank him, no matter what happens to us as a result, for having stayed with us, for having paid us this visit."
> "I feel the same way," her husband answered quickly. They looked at each other in surprise, with a new, and to them hitherto unknown, mutual understanding.*

In providing refuge for the escapee, Dr. and Mrs. Kress risked their lives. In doing so, however, they discovered a new sense of closeness with each other. By becoming involved in the risk of defying the authorities, they found themselves responding to each other in a new light. It was as if they had rediscovered the meaning of life by being willing to give up their lives for someone in need. In a personal way they had discovered what Jesus had declared, that life is found when it is willingly given up.

Just as George Heisler touched the lives of those who participated in his escape, so his escape touched the lives of the prisoners who remained. Anna Segher states her conviction in the closing words of the novel. She puts the words in the mouth of one of the remaining prisoners on the day in which the commandant had recognized defeat and had ordered the seventh empty cross removed.

> . . . All of us felt how ruthlessly and fearfully outward powers could strike to the very core of man, but at the same time we felt that at the very core there was something that was unassailable and inviolable.*

Heisler's successful escape challenged the remaining prisoners in the depth of their being. In reawakening their hope it reasserted their dignity as human beings whose lives counted. It challenged them with a task—to live as responsible human beings even in the concentration camp.

The call to responsibility is at the heart of any meaningful task. (*S/R*, 75.) It lay at the center of Schweitzer's mission into Africa. It was central to Peter's ministry. In the recorded account of Peter's encounter with Jesus following the resurrection, the message was very clear: "Get busy." Repeated three times, the admonition to "feed my sheep" (John 21:15-17) puts the challenge to responsible living very directly.

■ Display pictures of Affluent Woman (Resource Packet, item 8) and Negro Woman (Resource Packet, item 9). See the Leaders' Guide for detailed direction for their use.

Discuss as a group: How could a meaningful faith open a channel of achievement for these two women? What resources are in the faith to help these persons find meaning? Read in unison "O Young and Fearless Prophet" (*S/R*, 74).

Have one person read aloud while others follow the text or each person may read silently *S/R*, 72. How would a knowledge of Frankl's experience help the Negro woman face her situation? How could she learn about it? Read the prayer by Malcolm Boyd (*S/R*, 75).

In what ways does a meaningful faith challenge us to strive for achievement? How does a meaningful faith help us find a sense of worth and competence?

■ Close the session by praying together the "Prayer of Saint Francis" (Resource Packet, item 3).

■ Take the necessary assignments for through-the-week study.

NOTES ON CHAPTER 5

Page 83: Arthur Miller, *Death of a Salesman* (Viking Press, 1949), page 126. Copyright 1949 by Arthur Miller. Used by permission of the publisher.

Page 84: *Death of a Salesman*, pages 137-39. Used by permission.

Pages 88-89: Theodore Rubin, *Jordi; Lisa and David* (Ballantine Books, 1962), page 105. Used by permission of Macmillan Company.

Page 89: Isabel Smith, *Wish I Might* (Harper and Row, 1955), pages 64-65. Used by permission.

Page 90: Anna Seghers, *The Seventh Cross* (Little, Brown and Company, 1942), pages 330-31.

Page 90: *The Seventh Cross*, page 338.

Genesis 37:1-36
Joseph is sold into slavery. (*S/R,* 76.)

Genesis 39:1-23
Joseph is thrown into prison.

Luke 2:1-52
Jesus stays behind in the temple.

(*Read these selections in your Bible.*)

6
□□

A SEPARATE PERSON

At the weekly conference of the staff with the boss, Archibald as usual felt he had little to contribute. It was hard for him to think through his own thoughts and take a stand. Most of the time he waited to hear from the boss before he gave an opinion, and then it was usually in the form of a question rather than an original idea. He didn't like this in himself, but he never could seem to come up with anything new. It always made Imogene irritated with him when he waited until almost everyone else had spoken. She never really understood his feelings. His ideas never seemed to him to be as good as the others. Others on the staff were so definite about what they thought. He never could be so sure as they were. Perhaps he didn't really know what he thought.

When Biff, in *Death of a Salesman,* said of Willy, his father: "He never knew who he was," * the tragedy of Willy's

---

■ *As you arrive at your place of meeting, check the assignment chart for specific preparation to be made before the session begins.*

life is revealed. Some, like Willy, never discover who they are but go through life trying to be like someone else. For them, the identity question—the question of "who am I?"— is never answered and little happiness is known. Willy's suicide was a logical result.

Self-discovery comes slowly for most people and for some, like Willy, only in occcasional moments. Joseph in the biblical story came to know himself only gradually. The Joseph story tells of a favored son, whose mark of favor, a special coat, so aroused his brothers' jealousy that they plotted against his life. The hardships they created, however, eventually led to his growth. Our first glimpse of Joseph is of a spoiled child who took himself too seriously and who saw himself in an unlikable, self-centered way. Separated from his over-protective father, sold into slavery by his jealous brothers, tempted by a faithless wife in the king's palace (Genesis 39:1-23), he was forced to develop a personality of his own.

SELF-DISCOVERY

Although Archibald disliked problems as much as anyone, he had to admit that most of his growth had come by working through difficulties. He often surprised himself by what he was able to accomplish. Much of the time he was able to do far more than he thought he could. It made him realize that he really didn't know himself very well. (S/R, 77.)

William James, an American psychologist, said that most people make little use of their abilities. He said that people are like the man who gets in the habit of using only a little finger when he could make use of his whole body. James was convinced that most people live a very narrow life when compared with what they might do. He uses the figure of speech of the runner's "second wind." * When the runner pushes on against the first feelings of fatigue, he suddenly experiences a sense of release, a new freedom to run, the "second wind." Most people, James claims, never push beyond the first feelings of being tired and so never know the release of the "second wind." (*S/R,* 78.) Most people never discover their real potential.

For some, self-discovery comes very slowly. Ibsen's play *A Doll's House* tells of a wife, Nora, who has been so sheltered by her husband that she is no longer a woman living in a home but is like a doll living in a doll house. Her announcement to her husband, Torvald, that she is leaving him is her declaration of independence, her coming to herself.

Nora. ". . . You have always been so kind to me. But our home has been nothing but a playroom. I have been your doll-wife, just as at home I was papa's doll-child; and here the children have been my dolls. I thought it great fun when you played with me, just as they thought it great fun when I played with them. That is what our marriage has been, Torvald."

. . . .

"I must stand quite alone, if I am to understand myself and everything about me. It is for that reason that I cannot remain with you any longer!"

Torvald. "Nora, Nora!"

Nora. "I am going away from here now, at once. . . ."

Torvald. "You are out of your mind! I won't allow it! I forbid you!"

Nora. "It is no use forbidding me anything any longer. I will take with me what belongs to myself. I will take nothing from you, either now or later."

Torvald. "What sort of madness is this!" *

It seems like madness to Torvald, but Nora's need to know herself is so great that she has to leave her husband to achieve it. Her need to be seen as a real person is echoed by Willy Loman when, in *Death of a Salesman,* he objects to the statement made by his son, Biff:

Biff. "Pop! I'm a dime a dozen, and so are you!"

Willy. *Turning on him now is an uncontrolled outburst:* "I am not a dime a dozen! I am Willy Loman, and you are Biff Loman!" *

To insist on being a real person, distinctive, separate, and unique is to be human! Willy's insistence on being taken as an individual is in sharp contrast to Franz Kafka's portrayal of another salesman. In a frightening parable, Kafka portrays a typical salesman who lives an uninspired, routine, middle-class life.* He eats the same roast beef dinner every Sunday with the same father who leads an equally empty life. In the parable the salesman wakes up one morning to find that he has changed into a cockroach, a parasite who lives off the leftovers of others. In this powerful story the author is saying that the man who hasn't fulfilled his being gives up his manhood. He becomes something less than human, something objectionable and undesirable.

Neither Biff nor Happy, Willy's two sons in *Death of a Salesman,* has grown up. Happy can't face any truth. He lives in a kind of dream world of irresponsible relationships with one woman after another. Biff remains the perpetual adolescent. He thinks of himself in terms of his former glory as an athlete. His mother says sadly to him: "Biff, a man is not a bird, to come and go with the springtime." * Her disappointment only drives him farther from growing up, for it only accents his own dislike for himself.

Erik Erikson, a well-known student of personality development, believes the identity crisis (coming to an understanding of "Who am I?") comes in late adolescence. (*S/R,* 79.) When identity is not established in the teen years, a "confusion of role" results that leads to continuous adolescent-like behavior. If the person does not come to a mature understanding of who he is, he remains an adolescent in behavior and outlook. This pattern is demonstrated in *Death of a Salesman* by Biff, the athlete son who has never been able to hold a job and who is in constant tension with his father. Linda, his mother, is talking with him:

Linda. ". . . Why are you so hateful to each other? Why is that?"
Biff.   "I'm not hateful, Mom."
Linda. "But you no sooner come in the door than you're fighting."
Biff.   "I don't know why. I mean to change. I'm tryin', Mom, you understand?"
Linda. "Are you home to stay now?"
Biff.   "I don't know. I want to look around, see what's doin'."

Linda.   "Biff, you can't look around all your life, can you?"

Biff.   "I just can't take hold, Mom. I can't take hold of some kind of a life."

Linda.   "Biff, a man is not a bird, to come and go with the springtime."

Biff.   "Your hair . . . Your hair got so gray." *

Erikson suggests that identity involves both the accomplished experiences that have made a person feel significant in the past *and* the anticipated experiences that loom up ahead in which others see him playing a significant role. Biff's problem is that neither the past nor the future gives him a clear perception of himself.

■ Set goals for your study of this chapter as suggested on pages 15-16.

■ You will need Bibles for all members of the group and enough Methodist hymnals for every two persons. Have one member of the class tell the story of Joseph as found in Genesis 37:1-36 and 39:1-23. Discuss Joseph's experiences in the light of Archibald's claim that "growth had come by working through difficulties." See also S/R, 81 and Hebrews 12. In what other areas of life may growth come through difficulty?

■ Let each person read silently Psalms 8 from the Bible or as S/R, 77. Compare the psalmist's view of man with that expressed by some of the well-known hymns. See *The Methodist Hymnal* (1966), pages 415, 417, and 418.

Discuss: What is the worth of man according to the psalmist? According to the hymn writer? Which view do you hold? Why? How might the words of the psalm bear out the fact that most people never really discover their potential? Read in unison a hymn writer's version of Psalms 8. See page 41 or 44, *The Methodist Hymnal.*

■ Have two persons read the dialogue between Nora and Torvald from *A Doll's House* (page 95). In pairs discuss: How would you state or explain what Nora was feeling? Do you ever feel as she did? What is your idea of a real person? Suppose Nora had not left Torvald, how could she have achieved self-identity in her situation? When are you confused about your identity? Describe a person you consider to be distinctive, separate, real.

■ Have one person read aloud S/R, 79, and others follow the text. How does this help one understand the behavior and attitudes of adolescents and young adults?

■ One member of the class who, earlier, was assigned the task of interviewing a medical doctor or a psychiatrist may report his findings. The report will deal with these questions: How is the individual affected mentally and emotionally if he has no experiences of past accomplishments? How will he react toward the present and the future?

BECOMING INDEPENDENT

When lunch time came, Archibald debated phoning his father to have lunch with him. He had an important decision to make. Archibald felt very secure when he saw his father. The older man was so firmly established in life. But Archibald decided against making the call. His freedom had been hard to come by. It hadn't been easy to assert his independence when his father lived right there in the same town. In fact, he still was inclined to make decisions like his father did. Imogene had helped to make the break. She had made it clear to her in-laws, in a pleasant but firm way, that she and Archibald had to live life their own way. Whenever Archibald had been tempted to fall back into the dependent son attitude, Imogene had given the encouragement needed to stand firm. As he headed for the cafeteria, Archibald only hoped he could be big enough to let his own children grow away from him. (S/R, 80.)

The first requirement for maturity is a freedom from emotional dependence on a parent. Countless marriages have been broken over this issue, and countless lives have been made miserable at this point. I recall one young professional woman of about thirty who sought counseling because her life was so "dull." She always adjusted herself to everyone else's point of view, and she was completely dominated by her mother's wishes. When her mother would send her fudge, she would eat it all even though she was trying to lose weight. When her mother bought her clothes, she always wore them even though her tastes were very different from her mother's.

In our culture, making a break from parents often comes at the time of going away to college. For many, an actual separation in distance is a real aid toward achieving independence. If Joseph in the biblical story had stayed at home, he would have had a hard time severing the close ties with which his father's indulgent love bound him. Even though his brothers' intentions were bad, they accomplished a good result. By selling Joseph into slavery, they sent him far from home, broke the ties of dependence, and set him free to develop his own life. He recognized the usefulness of what they had done, declaring that God's hand had been in it. (S/R, 81.)

Shakespeare's Hamlet expresses the striving for independence in a famous speech as he poses the question, "To be or not to be." * "To be" means to be loyal to himself, to the standards that he holds to be true, to the people whose love he cherishes. "Not to be" means to live a living death. Shakespeare was right in presenting Hamlet's question in relationship to his parents, for the question of being oneself is first solved with the parents. For Hamlet, to be loyal to himself meant to turn against his parents. (S/R, 82.)

In the New Testament there is a story that describes the problem of the adolescent who is searching for meaning. It is the parable of the two sons and the father who wanted them to work in his vineyard (Matthew 21:28-31). The parable was probably meant to distinguish between lip service and actual devotion, but it describes the reactions of a rebellious adolescent. Each son was told to go to work. The first said he would not but later went. The second said he would go but then didn't go. Here are two radically different responses to the same demand. The first son asserted his own individuality by refusing simply to give in to his father's demand. Having asserted his independence, however, he then chose to carry out the order. But it was a deliberate choice. The second son, on the other hand, gave quick verbal assent to the order but never carried it out. He could not rebel openly, but he rebelled nevertheless. Each son declared his independence but only the first son did it in a healthy way.

Erikson reminds us that the adolescent has a new identity to establish that is different from his identity as a child. The new identity is called forth by the new commitments that the adolescent has to make. It is furthered by the new choices offered to the adolescent's recently matured body. It is given form by the new opportunities that the adult world sets forth. In the exhilarating experience of being on his own, the older adolescent creates his new identity by the new roles that he undertakes. The fact that he is asked to establish a new identity in a world in which everything is in flux only intensifies his problem. To offer to him new and demanding loyalties is one of the opportunities of the adult world. (*S/R*, 83.)

■ Look again at Genesis 37. Suppose Joseph's brothers had not sold him into slavery, what kind of an adult might he have come to be? How important was crisis to his development?

■ Two persons may be prepared to read aloud *S/R*, 82 and 83. Another may read Matthew 21:28-31.

Discuss in the total group: How can parents help youth sever the ties of dependence? How can youth be helped to have a positive picture of themselves? How can parents help youth see that there *is* a choice to be made? What is your response to the idea that it is more important to teach a young person that he has the power to choose than to teach him how to behave?

Perhaps you could have a panel discussion by three or four youth in response to this section of the material.

SELECTING A NEW LOYALTY

Standing in line at the cafeteria, Archibald realized how glad he was that he had not called his father. He had a decision to make, and he knew he had to make it by himself. He knew what his father would say. His father's way was always legally correct. It seemed to Archibald, however, that personal values were at stake that counted for more than simply legality. It was a matter of staying with the letter of the law or of following its spirit. His reading of the New Testament faith made it clear to him that the spirit was what counted. Indeed, in his own struggle toward maturity, the guiding principle for him was the spirit of Jesus. His faith required a new kind of loyalty. Archibald hoped that the day would come when he could hold firmly to his new loyalty and disagree openly with his father.

If self-discovery is a matter of letting go the childlike patterns of the past, it is also a matter of taking on new loyalties for the future. The episode of twelve-year-old Jesus in the temple at Jerusalem illustrates the change that takes place in the adolescent's life. (Read Luke 2:41-52.) For Jesus a new and greater loyalty had taken the place of loyalty to his parents. (*S/R,* 84.) His parents were not aware of his growing up. They hadn't realized that he was interested in adult concerns. To their rebuke about their anxieties when they couldn't find him, Jesus simply replied: "How is it that you sought me? Did you not know that I must be in my Father's house?"

The Old Testament account of Joseph is the story of the change from dependence on an earthy father (Jacob) to dependence on God. The writer of the Joseph narrative points out how "the LORD was with Joseph," but Joseph was the one who chose to make God's will his way. When Joseph finally greets Jacob in a family reunion, it is a remaking of the ties of love between two adults. Each had established his own unique identity.

When the transition is made from loyalty to the family and its way of life to larger loyalties, several possible pathways are open. The most tempting road is that of secularism, of putting the values of a success-oriented culture in first place. (*S/R,* 85.) As we have already seen, it was Willy Loman's downfall to place such a high priority on secular values. He lost sight of the virtues of honesty and integrity that had made him a lovable person.

Willy's successful uncle, Ben, represents the secular pathway. He appears over and over again in the play, but he is always in a hurry, always about to leave to catch a train. He boasts of having walked into the "jungle" as a boy of seventeen and of walking out as a rich man at the age of twenty-one. His advice to Biff is: "Never fight fair with a stranger, boy. You'll never get out of the jungle that way." * Ben encourages Willy to commit suicide because it will mean income from insurance for Linda and the boys. Linda withdraws from Ben and is frightened by him. She sees in him a false set of values. She knows that money isn't everything and that Willy in his lovable ways is a far more attractive person than Ben in his hard-headed, realistic, wealthy way.

The temptation to secularism is hard to resist in our culture where so much attention is given to material things. Biff's brother, Happy, however, in his better moments sees the fallacy of a life built on things:

> "All I can do now is wait for the merchandise manager to die. And suppose I get to be merchandise manager? He's a good friend of mine, and he just built a terrific estate on Long Island. And he lived there about two months and sold it, and now he's building another one. He can't enjoy it once it's finished. And I know that's just what I would do. I don't know what . . . I'm workin' for. Sometimes I sit in my apartment—all alone. And I think of the rent I'm paying. And it's crazy. But then, it's what I always wanted. My own apartment, a car, and plenty of women. And still, . . . I'm lonely." *

Of course, Happy is lonely. His loneliness will never be satisfied as long as things have a more important place in his life than persons. Man cannot live by bread alone or by cars and women. Meaning is found not in things but in responsible relationships. The New Testament is very clear about the need for finding worthwhile loyalties. Real freedom comes when a release from childlike patterns makes possible the taking on of adult ways. And the adult way is the way of service, the way of love. "The whole law," Paul wrote, "is fulfilled in one word, 'You shall love your neighbor as yourself' " (Galatians 5:14).

One of my acquaintances is a psychiatrist who left a very successful private practice to enter public service. The move cut his salary actually in half. But he says it is worth it! He is finding far greater satisfaction in meaningful service in community preventive mental health than he ever found with his wealthy private patients.

A second pathway that is hard to resist is the way of popularity, of doing things that others want you to do. Willy puts it in terms of being liked. He and his sons are talking together about a neighbor, Bernard.

Willy.   "Bernard is not well liked, is he?"
Biff.   "He's liked, but he's not well liked."
Happy.   "That's right, Pop."

Willy.   "That's just what I mean. Bernard can get the best
           marks in school, y'understand, but when he gets out in
           the business world, y'understand, you are going to be
           five times ahead of him. That's why I thank Almighty
           God you're both built like Adonises. Because the man
           who makes an appearance in the business world, the
           man who creates personal interest, is the man who gets
           ahead. Be liked and you will never want. You take me,
           for instance. I never had to wait in line to see a buyer.
           'Willy Loman is here!' That's all they have to know, and
           I go right through."
Biff.   "Did you knock them dead, Pop?"
Willy.   "Knocked 'em cold in Providence, slaughtered 'em in
           Boston." *

The tragedy, of course, is that "being well liked" wasn't
enough for Willy. A person is really liked, not for what he
does but for what he is. Willy was a slave to the popularity
cult. He knew nothing of the sense of freedom that the Christian faith talks about. The slavery to the "elemental spirits
of the universe" (Galatians 4:3) that Paul speaks of is the
kind of slavery that Willy knew. In his need to be popular,
he was bound as surely as if his hands and feet were tied.
Popularity leads to the kind of conformity in which principles give way to the pressures of the moment. (S/R, 86.)

One of the characteristic traits of mature persons is that
they are inner-directed. Like Joseph who determined his
way of behavior by inner principle rather than by outer pressures, the mature person risks momentary unpopularity to
stand by his convictions. The history of progress of freedom
in the world is the story of men and women of conviction
who chose martyrdom rather than yield their principles. In
Martyr's Square in Oxford, England, there is a monument to
the memory of the English Bishops Latimer and Ridley who
were burned there at the stake on October 6, 1555, because of
their Protestant beliefs. They were bound with heavy chains
to a post of iron. Latimer turned to Ridley as the fagots were
lit and spoke words that have echoed down through the cor-
ridors of time: "Be of good cheer, Master Ridley, play the
man; we shall this day light such a candle, by God's grace,

in England, as I trust shall never be put out." Even though bound, they were free spirits. Their total commitment made them free.

A third challenge to the loyalty of a person who is moving from the shelter of home to the broader areas of life is the attraction of certainty. This way presents itself in many forms. Sometimes it is the certainty of science in which every fact has a determining cause and every event has a foreseeable outcome. Sometimes it is the certainty of a totalitarian form of government in which individual freedom is given up for the security of being told how to think and how to act. Sometimes it is an absolute way of thinking, a closed system of belief in which the answers are prescribed in specific rules in a book.

In *Escape From Freedom,* Erich Fromm writes about the temptation to seek certainty at any price, even at the price of accepting the authority of a totalitarian state such as communism or Nazism. The appeal of any absolute system, whether it be a form of government or a way of thinking, is that it eliminates uncertainty. Everything is clear-cut, black or white. The argument advanced again and again by those Germans who participated in the mass murder of six million Jews under Hitler's National Socialism was that they were only carrying out their orders. Their only responsibility, they claimed, was to be loyal subjects, giving clear-cut obedience to clear-cut orders. Either they were loyal followers of their leader or they were not. The issue was black or white. (*S/R,* 87.)

However, very little is actually black or white. In the science of physics, for example, the concept of matter has undergone drastic changes. Rather than being viewed as something solid with a no-nonsense kind of firmness, matter is better understood as a fluid mass, a quantity of energy. The mass is characterized more by its atomic structure and its potential energy than by its dimensions or its color or its weight. Thus physics, thought to be the most exact of all sciences, turns out to be far from exact. Moreover, in the age of atomic energy, the need for thinking not only of how atomic power can be created but also of how it should be used makes it clear that physics cannot be considered apart from a philosophy of life.

Religion is not as exact as the sciences. If religion is to be thought of as the dimension in depth, as we have suggested before, then religious language must be a language that handles more than matters of fact. Much of the difficulty in religious thinking has grown out of the attempt to use factual terms to think religiously, when, in fact, religious thinking always calls for symbolic terms. (S/R, 88.) The whole Joseph saga is symbolic of God's care for his people. These records of life experiences transcend any particular time. The love of Jacob for the son of his old age, the jealousy of Joseph's brothers for the favored son, the temptation to seek sexual satisfaction outside marriage, the inclination to repay injustice with injustice—all these are a part of life that is not dependent on any particular time or place or culture.

Maturity calls for a change of sovereignty from a loyalty to family to wider loyalties. We have noted that there are competing claims for a person's loyalty and especially for a young person's loyalty. We have suggested that a persistent challenge comes from the secular culture to accept the standards of materialism or of hedonism in its self-centered, other-directed guise or of totalitarianism, whether in science or politics or religion. The real challenge to Christianity is that of so presenting a new loyalty to God that these other challenges fail to really attract.

When Jesus in his young manhood sorted out the temptations that confronted him, he found answers to them by referring in each instance to God. It was because of God that he would not turn stones into bread and satisfy his immediate personal needs. It was because of God that he would live out a life of service rather than one of power. It was because of God that he would accept responsibility for how his life would be lived without counting on others to take over for him. His life can be understood only in terms of a commitment so basic that all else fell into place. Once and for all he established his ties of loyalty. His Father God replaced his earthly father.

■ Read aloud in unison Luke 2:41-52 and Mark 3:31-35. In each case Jesus is recognizing that his loyalty is to One greater than his family. He is moving from family loyalty to larger loyalties. See also *S/R*, 80 and 84.

Divide the class into three groups to discuss the pathways open to one when transition is made from family loyalty to larger loyalties.

Group A will study the section that deals with *secularism* (pages 101-2). Major ideas to talk about: success in terms of material things (*S/R*, 69); false sets of values; finding worthwhile loyalties; the adult way is a way of service; meaning is found, not in things but in relationships.

Group B will study the section that deals with *popularity* (pages 102-3). Major ideas to talk about: doing what others want you to do; one is liked for what he is, not what he does; lacking sense of freedom; danger of conformity (*S/R*, 87); inner-directed versus other-directed; maturity involves standing by convictions; freedom in total commitment.

Group C will study the section on *certainty* (pages 104-5). Major ideas to talk about: certainty through science, totalitarian form of government, absolute way of thinking; freedoms you give up for certainty; nothing is black or white; need for understanding religious language as symbolic (*S/R*, 88).

■ In the total group, discuss: In the light of the discussions regarding secularism, popularity, and certainty, how can Christianity challenge persons to give their loyalty to God rather than to these? Can the church as it now exists successfully combat them? What changes in it and in us may be necessary?

■ Pray together the "Prayer of Saint Francis" (Resource Packet, item 3).

■ Take the necessary assignments for through-the-week study.

NOTES ON CHAPTER 6

Page 93: Arthur Miller, *Death of a Salesman* (Viking Press, 1949), page 138. Copyright 1949 by Arthur Miller. Used by permission of the publisher.

Page 94: William James, *Memories and Studies* in *Selected Papers on Philosophy* (Everyman's Library, E. P. Dutton and Company, 1917), pages 40-41.

Page 95: Henrik Ibsen, *A Doll's House, The Wild Duck, and The Lady From the Sea* (E. P. Dutton and Company, Everyman's Library Edition, 1910), pages 69-70. Translated by R. F. Sharp and E. Marx-Aveling. Used by permission.

Page 95: *Death of a Salesman,* page 132. Used by permission.

Page 96: Franz Kafka, "Metamorphosis" in Charles Neider, editor, *Short Novels of the Masters* (Holt, Rinehart and Winston, 1948), pages 537-79.

Page 96: *Death of a Salesman,* page 54. Used by permission.

Pages 96-97: *Death of a Salesman,* page 54. Used by permission.

Page 99: Compare Erik H. Erikson, *Insight and Responsibility* (W. W. Norton and Company, 1964), page 125: Hamlet "demonstrates in word and deed that to him 'to be' is contingent on being loyal (to the self, to love, to the crown) and that the rest is death." Used by permission.

Page 101: *Death of a Salesman,* page 49. Used by permission.

Page 102: *Death of a Salesman,* page 23. Used by permission.

Pages 102-3: *Death of a Salesman,* page 33. Used by permission.

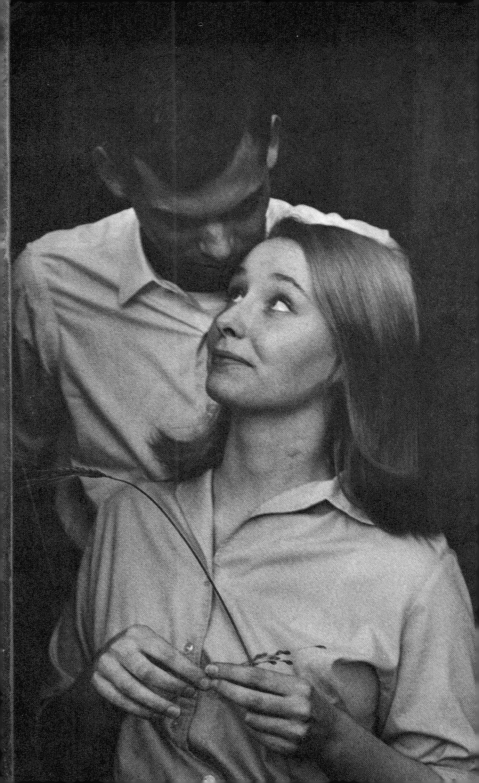

Luke 10:38-42
Jesus shares his concerns with Mary. (S/R, 89.)

1 Samuel 20:1-42
The friendship of David and Jonathan.

(Read these selections in your Bible.)

7

□□

SPEAKING WITH THE SECOND VOICE

It wasn't Archibald's custom to eat alone. As soon as he saw Irving, his friend in the sales department, he motioned to the empty chair beside him. As Irving approached, Archibald realized how much Irving's friendship meant to him. He was able to share some things with Irving that he couldn't talk about with anyone else except Imogene. Sometimes Imogene would say with a chuckle that Irving was like a counselor to Archibald. But it was better than that. Irving was such an open sort of person that it was easy to be open with him. Because Irving never played a part, Archibald didn't need to, either. Both men could be themselves without any pretending.

One of the choices each person constantly makes is to decide how much of himself he will share. One way to sense how hard it is for most people to share themselves is to observe what goes on in counseling. Even with the intent of

---

■ *As you arrive at your place of meeting, check the assignment chart for specific preparation to be made before the session begins.*

complete sharing and even when the counseling is paid for, the tendency is to withhold the true facts from the counselor. It is commonplace to try to present the best possible picture, even to the point of coloring the facts. Because no one likes to appear in a bad light, even the counselor tends to get a false picture. It is very hard to share openly all that one really is.

Yet, one of the greatest needs of our culture is to find someone who can be a real friend, in whom any confidences can be shared. (S/R, 90.) One counselor reports that many who have sought his help have told him: "You are the first person I have ever been completely honest with." * Arthur Miller's play *After the Fall* struggles with the need for more open sharing, especially between husband and wife. When Quentin is talking with his wife, Louise, with whom communication is particularly poor, he tries to express his desire to share himself freely with her:

> "I walked in just now—and I had a tremendous wish to come out—to you. And you to me. It sounds absurd that this city is full of people rushing to meet one another, Louise. This city is full of lovers." *

Louise treats his words as absurd and does not hear his desire for greater openness with her.

Whether with the counselor, or in marriage, or with friends, the need to share is very real. (S/R, 91.) From my perspective as a religious psychologist, I see the story of Mary and Martha in Bethany in a special light. For me, this story tells of a woman who had enough insight to sense that Jesus needed to confide in someone, to share his hopes and fears and joys and doubts. Mary was such a person. Ahead of Jesus lay Jerusalem, the center of opposition to his message. Relaxing in the comfort of the home of friends in Bethany, his real need was for conversation with someone with whom he could open his heart. Like most leaders, he knew the loneliness of leadership.

■ Set goals for your study of this chapter as suggested on pages 15-16.)

SELF-DISCOVERY THROUGH SHARING

As he talked with Irving, Archibald realized how free he felt. With Irving he never needed to pretend that he was someone he wasn't. He felt accepted as he was and in some way confirmed in the kind of person he was. The result was that he never felt the need to defend his actions. Because he didn't have to justify his behavior, he was freer to be critical of it, to learn from it, to think through other possibilities. By sharing with Irving, he was discovering more about himself than he knew was there.

Like Archibald, most of us need help in breaking down the barriers that cover over the real person. We have learned to hide our feelings. (*S/R*, 92.) Most of us have had much of our natural, spontaneous feeling trained out of us. Much of the appeal of children is that they are so natural, so free to say what they feel. When Jesus said, "Unless you turn and become like children, you will never enter the kingdom of heaven" (Matthew 18:3), he was thinking perhaps of this need for naturalness. A major contribution of counseling has been in pointing out the need to recognize feelings actually present before any steps can be taken to modify them.

■ Two persons read the Counseling Session (Resource Packet, item 15) aloud as dialogue. Discuss in small groups: Can we admit this kind of mixture of love and hate in ourselves? How can the mixture of love and hate in us be brought into the open *here in this group* in ways that will strengthen our feeling of unity? (See *S/R*, 90.)

I recall a patient in a mental hospital where I served as chaplain who interrupted a Sunday morning worship service while I was preaching. I was talking about the need for loving relationships when she stood up in the congregation and declared: "That's not what my doctor tells me." I put aside my sermon notes and spent the rest of the sermon period in a dialogue with her, across the congregation. I knew that other patients would be more interested in my comments to her than in my prepared sermon. Her point was that her doctor was trying to help her to accept the fact that she had many angry feelings about her parents. He was encouraging her to express these feelings, knowing that until she admitted them to herself there was little hope of her handling them. She was quite correct in stopping me. There was a task for her to accomplish *before* she could carry on the relationships in love that I had been talking about. She had to discover some things about her own true feelings before she could move on beyond them. Her discovery of herself was developing as she shared her feelings with the doctor, feelings that she had kept hidden even from herself for a long time.

■ Use the Christian Group Life check list (Resource Packet, item 16). Discuss points D, E, F, G, H. The Leaders' Guide in the packet will suggest a variety of uses for this item.

Any minister knows how important sharing is at the time of bereavement. In order for the feeling of loss to be faced and accepted, it must first be expressed. The expression of sorrow, however, is usually complicated by the fact that emotions are never pure. Any feeling is mixed. Love is never only love. It has some not-love involved in it. Sorrow is never only sorrow; it has some sense of relief or release in it, too. But it is extremely difficult for most people to acknowledge that their feelings are mixed. And our culture makes it all the more difficult. At the time of death, feelings of love are expressed with encouragement from the culture, but feelings of not-love are generally not acceptable. The result is that all feelings are often withheld. The following clinical notes from an actual bereavement situation show how mixed ("ambivalent") feelings are and how sharing all the feelings is necessary if the grief is to be handled. Notice how the grief-stricken parishioner tried to evade speaking of her feelings.

A minister was informed of the death of a man in the parish and went immediately to the home of the widow. He arrived there within two hours of the death. He found a woman of sixty-five who greeted him warmly. She seemed under great tension but did not speak of her husband's death

until he introduced the subject. He asked about the husband,
Joe, whom he had never met.

Widow.	"He was a fine man, a fine man. No one ever had a better husband. He did his best to provide for his family. When there was money in the house, a more generous man never existed. . . . We lived on a farm, you know."
Minister.	"Did you enjoy your years on the farm?"
Widow.	"Oh, I never minded them. They were good properties and we made a good living then. But we left the farm after the '29 crash came."
Minister.	"Those must have been difficult years for many people."
Widow.	"They were, and we were no exception. That's when I had to go to work. I'm a lab technician, you know. I've been working ever since."
Minister.	"Joe had difficulty after the depression, then?"
Widow.	"Difficulty isn't the word for it. . . . I hated the trouble we had after '29. I think I blamed Joe for that trouble. He just couldn't get going after the crash. That's why I had to go to work."
Minister.	"It bothered you to work?"
Widow.	"Well, I like the lab work, but I felt he should take care of us."
Minister.	"You felt resentful of having to assume a good share of the breadwinning."
Widow.	"That's it. I felt it was his job. He did it before '29, why not now. But no, he fooled around with insurance and never got anywhere. He lost it in deals faster than he made it."
Minister.	"You were married a long time. Were you and your husband happy together?"
Widow.	"Oh yes." (Spoken softly, then with a sob:) "No. I mean no." (She cried softly for a moment.) "I loved my husband, always have. He was a fine man. But in some ways I almost hated him at the same time. It's funny you love someone and then you almost hate him, too."
Minister.	"You are confused about feelings toward your husband?"
Widow.	"Yes, and what makes it so bad now is that I knew he knew it. When he lay there dying, he just looked at me and didn't say a word. I didn't either. We just looked at each other. I wish I'd said I was sorry or something. But somehow I couldn't. Now, even though I felt this about his supporting us, I love him. I miss

him. I wish he hadn't gone. But I still can't help feeling cheated."

Because this widow was helped to share her true feelings
about her husband, she could accept his death. Accepting
death, she could then face life assured that God is the Lord of
both death and life. By expressing the mixture of love and
hate, so typical in any human relationship, she was prepar-
ing herself for a new life in the future. By discovering and
admitting her real feelings, she was making her own growth
possible.

Self-discovery through sharing can never be compelled,
although it can be encouraged. A good deal of harm has
been done in the Christian community by people who said
they were "speaking the truth in love" (Ephesians 4:15). Too
often "speaking the truth" means direct criticism. The kind
of sharing we have in mind has more to do with the self
than with others. (S/R, 93.) Whereas passing judgment on
someone else seldom leads to anything constructive, sharing
personal feelings opens the way to more genuine communication. There is a considerable difference between telling
someone off ("You make me mad") and sharing feelings ("I
feel angry inside").

■ List some times we typically pretend to agree or support a person
rather than tell the disagreeable truth. How can we tell which we
are doing? Is there any time when one is better than the other? In
this connection, do you get any insight from S/R, 93?

PERSONAL SHARING IS DIFFICULT

Archibald was surprised at how much progress he had
made in sharing his feelings. He knew it was largely due to
Imogene. She never belittled anything he said about himself
but always accepted it as a fact. Because she was so accepting,
he had dared to share more and more. He knew that his marriage was stronger than most because he and Imogene could
share so much together. And he knew that he was freer with
Irving because he was so free with Imogene.

In many years of professional counseling I have never met

a couple who were completely satisfied with their relationship together. Most couples express their situation as one in which they don't seem to share much that really counts. A similar situation exists in most families. It is certainly commonplace for teen-agers to seek adults outside the family in whom they can confide. Anne Frank, a fifteen-year-old girl who hid with her family from Nazi persecution in a secret annex of a Dutch home, kept a diary during the days of hiding. She tells of how her family failed her by not allowing her to share what was going on in her:

> "When I was in difficulties you all closed your eyes and stopped up your ears and didn't help me; on the contrary, I received nothing but warnings not to be so boisterous. I was only boisterous so as not to be miserable all the time. I was reckless so as not to hear that persistent voice within me continually. . . ." *

When her parents failed her, Anne found someone who understood her in seventeen-year-old Peter. He was also in hiding. Like many adolescents, she found help toward greater self-discovery by sharing her inner thoughts with someone in her own age group. The biblical story of David's friendship with Jonathan is a good example of how understanding is found best in a friend in the same age group.

> ■ Continue, but *in pairs,* to discuss points raised in previous discussion. Let each person practice repeating what his partner is saying to the partner's satisfaction before replying ("Are you saying . . . "?) . Practice trying to overcome the barriers to understanding and to hearing each other. After two or three exchanges, read *S/R, 94.* What does this reading suggest to us about the *reasons* for such barriers?

We are all familiar with how hard it is to say what we really are thinking. Young people often find it easier to talk with each other than with adults, but it isn't always so. A young nurse tells of caring for a patient in the terminal stages of cancer. He was dying, and she knew it. She felt guilty to be in such vigorous health when he, at about her age, was dying. She reported her feelings to a social worker:

"I know he wanted to talk to me; but I always turned it into something light, a little joke, or into some evasive reassurance which had to fail. The patient knew and I knew. But, as he saw my desperate attempts to escape and felt my anxiety, he took pity on me and kept to himself what he wanted to share with another human being. And so he died and did not bother me." *

Anne Morrow Lindbergh writes in a similar way of the human tragedy of being unable to speak the appropriate word at the time it is needed. In her novel *Dearly Beloved,* the title of which is taken from the first two words of the traditional wedding ceremony, she tells of a mother's inability to share her deep feelings with her daughter. Deborah, the mother, is helping her daughter, Sally, to adjust her wedding veil.

Deborah went to her daughter, kissed her lightly on the forehead, and hesitated for a moment, looking urgently, almost pleading, into her wide eyes.

Wasn't there something she could say at this moment—mother to daughter—something real? Sally, too, seemed to be pleading, asking for some confirmation.

"Your father will be up—" Deborah blurted in a rush. All she could say. The words for good-by never came at the right moment. . . . The real thing never got said.*

To say the real thing is one of the driving concerns of the playwright Tennessee Williams. Many turn away from his plays because of the coarse language that he uses and because of the pessimism that is so apparent in much of his writing. An insight, however, is given in his preface to *Cat on a Hot Tin Roof* in which he writes of his own inability to share freely with people and of his desire to deal with the real thing that so seldom gets said. (*S/R,* 94.) Even the title of his preface is revealing: "Person—to—Person."

. . . A morbid shyness once prevented me from having much direct communication with people, and possibly that is why I began to write to them plays and stories. . . . I still find it somehow easier to "level with" crowds of strangers in the hushed twilight of orchestra and balcony sections of theatres than with individuals across a table from me. . . .

116

. . . I still don't want to talk to people only about the surface aspects of their lives, the sort of things that acquaintances laugh and chatter about on ordinary social occasions.*

. . . And so we talk to each other, write and wire each other, call each other short and long distance across land and sea, clasp hands with each other at meeting and at parting, fight each other and even destroy each other because of this always somewhat thwarted effort to break through walls to each other. . . .*

In the play that follows this preface, Tennessee Williams sets forth the efforts of Maggie, the wife, to break through the wall that separates her from her husband, Brick. The wall between them is only typical of the wall between all the members of the family. Each has surrounded himself with lies. These lies were originally designed to give protection from the hard truth but have eventually built walls isolating each from the other. The climactic scene comes in Act II when Big Daddy confronts his son, Brick.

■ Let two persons (an older and a younger, if possible) read aloud the passage below from *Cat on a Hot Tin Roof*. The readers need not be dramatic artists, but at least one previous reading will help them to interpret the lines. After the reading, *discuss in the same pairs* as suggested above: Have you ever really tried to express your true feelings as Brick and Big Daddy do here? What happened? What difference does it make if a parent and child are involved, even if the child is a young adult? How can such honesty occur in this church?

Brick describes their predicament nicely:

Brick. "Are you through talkin' to me?"
Big Daddy. "Why are you so anxious to shut me up?"
Brick. "Well, sir, ever so often you say to me, Brick, I want to have a talk with you, but when we talk, it never materializes. Nothing is said. You sit in a chair and gas about this and that and I look like I listen. I try to look like I listen, but I don't listen, not much. Communication is—awful hard between people an'—somehow between you and me, it just don't—" *

Big Daddy determines that communication is going to take place between them, hard as it is. In the scene that follows he pursues Brick relentlessly through all attempts at evasion. He won't let his son go until the truth is revealed. And in the process Brick, on his part, reveals the truth of his father's terminal illness to him. Big Daddy isn't satisfied with Brick's account of the death of his friend, Skipper.

Big Daddy. "Something's left out of that story. What did you leave out?" [*The phone has started ringing in the hall. As if it reminded him of something, Brick glances suddenly toward the sound and says:*]

Brick. "Yes!—I left out a long-distance call which I had from Skipper, in which he made a drunken confession to me and on which I hung up!—last time we spoke to each other in our lives. . . ."

Big Daddy. "You hung up?"

Brick. "Hung up. . . . Well—"

Big Daddy. "Anyhow now!—we have tracked down the lie with which you're disgusted and which you are drinking to kill your disgust with, Brick. You been passing the buck. This disgust with mendacity is disgust with yourself. *You!*—dug the grave of your friend and kicked him into it!—before you'd face truth with him!"

Brick. *"His truth, not mine!"*

Big Daddy. "His truth, okay! But you wouldn't face it with him!"

Brick. "Who *can* face truth? Can *you?*"

Big Daddy. "Now don't start passin' the rotten buck again, boy!"

Brick. *"How about these birthday congratulations, these many, many happy returns of the day, when ev'rybody but you knows there won't be any!"* *

So Brick tells his father that he is going to die. It is as if he can no longer stomach mendacity, that is, pretense and lying. "You told *me!*" Brick says, and "I told *you.*" *

This play of Tennessee Williams points out the cost of being willing to share the truth. Neither Brick nor Big Daddy wants to face the facts. Both go through agony in facing the truth, but both come out of it as stronger persons. They discover that they can live with the facts. They discover that when truth can be faced and shared, growth results.

118

We have been noting how easy it is for barriers to sharing to be erected. When Anne Frank writes: "I'm afraid they'll laugh at me, think I'm ridiculous and sentimental, not take me seriously," * she is giving a good reason for not sharing her more serious side. Erikson reminds us that young people need both "confirming adults and affirming peers." * Anne thought she did not have confirming adults, but she did find an affirming companion in Peter. She illustrates Erikson's thought that young people would prefer to talk instead of necking. She writes:

> Oh, yes, there's still so much I want to talk to him about, for I don't see the use of only just cuddling each other. To exchange our thoughts, that shows confidence and faith in each other, we would both be sure to profit by it! *

Falling in love, Erikson reminds us, is less a sexual matter for a young person than it is an attempt at a definition of one's identity. The process is one of "projecting one's diffused ego image on another and by seeing it thus reflected and gradually clarified." *

The difficulty Anne had in sharing her feelings with the adult world is not limited to adolescents. It is easy to understand middle-aged Quentin who becomes judgmental when he is uncertain. In *After the Fall* he says: "I do judge, and harshly, too—when the fact is I'm bewildered." * As is often the case, instead of sharing his bewilderment, he becomes all the more certain of his pronouncements.

One therapist, Sidney Jourard, writes of the need for "speaking with the second voice." * He models his phrase on Theodore Reik's classic words, "Listening with the third ear." Whereas Reik refers to listening for the unspoken meanings and the implied overtones, Jourard refers to the spontaneous comments that he is prompted to make. In contrast to therapists who ration their words carefully in order that everything they say may be therapeutic, Jourard says whatever he is prompted to say.

I find myself sometimes giving advice, lecturing, laughing, becoming angry, interpreting, telling my fantasies, asking questions —in short, doing whatever occurs to me *during* the therapeutic session in response to the other person.*

Jourard believes that his therapeutic effectiveness is enhanced now that he is freer to share. He believes that too many therapists have allowed technique to become a barrier between them and their patients. The implications of this point of view for teachers and for parents is quite apparent.

A COMMON FAITH ENCOURAGES SHARING

Archibald and Irving had a good deal in common. (*S/R*, 95.) They were about the same age, worked for the same firm, had families of similar size, and had wives who were congenial. Probably the most important factor, however, was their sharing of similar values. Although they talked little about their faith, their outlook on life was similar. It was rooted in a Christian system of values. They weren't too sure how important the church was in their lives, but they sensed that the church strengthened their belief about what was important. Their view of life was God-centered rather than man-centered.

The ability to share is often developed in crisis periods when a common need brings people closer together. Ernest Gordon has written an account of the horrors and the miracles of life in a prisoner-of-war camp in Thailand. In his autobiography called *Through the Valley of the Kwai,* he tells of his efforts to start a university in the camp. Any talent available was put to use. A lawyer told stories of famous trials. An architect conducted a course on designing a house. Yachtsmen lectured on building and sailing boats. Gordon himself held an evening reading session in which he read of the "problems, foibles, quirks, eccentricities, humors, and virtues of other people." * He helped the men to gain a deeper appreciation of themselves as members of the human race.

Gordon tells of one particular evening when the men felt drawn especially close to one another.

When I had finished my story for the night I was aware of a sense of kinship. We were human beings with the same puzzlements and the same hopes. We were being drawn toward a center that was beyond ourselves, a center that was good, that gave us cause to hope, that promised the fulfillment of life—a life that was joyously sweet.*

Gordon was an agnostic when he entered the death camp by the River Kwai. He was asked by the men to lead them in "another go at this Christianity" * to find out whether or not there might be something in it for them. In searching out answers for them, Gordon found answers for himself. He is today the Dean of the Chapel at Princeton University. He found the "center . . . that promised the fulfillment of life." * He tells of a conversation with a twenty-eight-year-old soldier whose illness and suffering made him look like an old man. The soldier is speaking:

"Do you know what I've come to think? There's a harmony about life. When you put yourself in tune with that harmony, you sense the rightness about things. You know a peace in your heart."

"You've found that peace, then?"

"Yes, I reckon I have. I used to gripe and complain about everything—about the Nips, the Government, my buddies, myself."

"Most of us have been feeling that way," I acknowledged.

"Maybe we have. But I bet I was one of the worst."

"How do you figure the change came about?" I asked.

"It came gradually," he said. "I learned to accept things—to accept the Nips and their awfulness. I accepted my mates. I accepted myself. Then I stopped griping so much and tried to do what I could to help. Every little bit I gave made me seem more at ease with. myself. I decided no matter what happens I've got to do what I believe to be right." *

Gordon ended the conversation by suggesting that what the soldier was trying to do was to do God's will. As he put it: "What seems to me important about a church is that we all come together as one when we open ourselves to God's will." * (S/R, 96 and 97.)

■ Read aloud S/R, 96 and 97. Contrast the main ideas of the two definitions of the church. What is the key difference? With which definition do you most nearly agree? In which kind of church would you rather serve? Why?

When people are facing in the same direction and when there is an openness to a common goal, then sharing comes more easily. Church groups have less of a problem with hostility than many other similar groups because a common loyalty is more important than the usual hostile feelings that are present. This was a part of the miracle on the River Kwai. A common search for God's will made lesser concerns seem unimportant. Being drawn to the same center, the men became more charitable with each other and opened their lives more to each other. (S/R, 98.)

■ Bring stories from your own experience or from television or movie viewing, or ideas from your reading, in which the search for God's will has overcome lesser concerns. (S/R, 98 is an interpretation of such experience.) Scriptural passages and prayers may be included. Let as many as possible share these items and their meaning to you.
■ Conclude with the "Prayer of Saint Francis" (Resource Packet, item 3).
■ How will you prepare for the next session?

NOTES ON CHAPTER 7

Page 110: Sidney M. Jourard, *The Transparent Self* (D. Van Nostrand Company, 1964), page iv. Copyright 1964 by D. Van Nostrand Company. Used by permission.

Page 110: Arthur Miller, *After the Fall* (Viking Press, 1964), page 61. Copyright © 1964 by Arthur Miller. Used by permission of the publisher.

Page 115: Anne Frank, *The Diary of a Young Girl* (Doubleday and Company, 1952), page 239. Copyright 1952 by Otto H. Frank. Used by permission of the publisher.

Page 116: Ilse S. Wolff, "The Magnificence of Understanding" in Samuel Standard and Helmuth Nathan, editors, *Should the Patient Know the Truth?* (Springer Publishing Company, 1955), page 32. Used by permission.

Page 116: Anne Morrow Lindbergh, *Dearly Beloved* (Harcourt, Brace and World, 1962), page 10. Used by permission.

Pages 116-17: Tennessee Williams, *Cat on a Hot Tin Roof* (New Directions Book, 1955), pages viii-ix. Copyright 1955 by Tennessee Williams. Used by permission of New Directions Publishing Corporation.

Page 117: *Cat on a Hot Tin Roof,* page vi. Used by permission.

Page 117: *Cat on a Hot Tin Roof,* page 74. Used by permission.

Page 118: *Cat on a Hot Tin Roof,* pages 108-9. Used by permission.

Page 118: *Cat on a Hot Tin Roof,* page 112. Used by permission.

Page 119: *The Diary of a Young Girl,* page 281. Used by permission.

Page 119: Erik H. Erikson, *Insight and Responsibility* (W. W. Norton and Company, 1964), page 125. Used by permission.

Page 119: *The Diary of a Young Girl,* pages 226-27. Used by permission.

Page 119: Erik H. Erikson, *Childhood and Society* (W. W. Norton and Company, 1964), page 262. Used by permission.

Page 119: *After the Fall,* page 60. Used by permission.

Page 119: *The Transparent Self,* page 69. Used by permission.

Page 120: *The Transparent Self,* page 69. Used by permission.

Page 120: Ernest Gordon, *Through the Valley of the Kwai* (Harper and Row, 1962), pages 205-6. Copyright 1962 by Ernest Gordon. Used by permission of the publisher.

Page 121: *Through the Valley of the Kwai,* page 206. Used by permission.

Page 121: *Through the Valley of the Kwai,* page 116. Used by permission.

Page 121: *Through the Valley of the Kwai,* page 206. Used by permission.

Page 121: *Through the Valley of the Kwai,* pages 206-7. Used by permission.

Pages 121-22: *Through the Valley of the Kwai,* page 207. Used by permission.

2 Corinthians 12:7-10
Paul finds strength in weakness. (S/R, 99.)

Acts 22:1-29
Paul tells of how he became a Christian.

Matthew 5:38-42
Turning the other cheek.

(Read these selections in your Bible.)

8
□□□
SEEING IN MY DARKNESS

Before going back to work, Archibald phoned Imogene.
There wasn't any particular reason. He just wanted to hear
her voice. As he put down the phone, he thought back over
their life together. The sense of intimacy that was theirs
had grown only gradually. Each had been pretty independent
when they had married. To give themselves completely to
each other hadn't been easy, and it still wasn't always possible, but they had come a long way together. He realized
that practically everything he did took on fresh meaning because of his relationship with Imogene. In a strange and
rather wonderful way, life had opened to him when he had
opened himself to her. By losing himself in her, he had found
himself. And because of her, he was freer to lose himself in
broader concerns.

Any athlete knows the experience of forgetting himself in
the running of a race. Any musician knows what it is to lose

■ *As you arrive at your place of meeting, check the assignment chart for
specific preparation to be made before the session begins.*

himself in the playing of a great symphony. Any scientist knows how individual interests can be forgotten in the search for a new discovery. Any student knows how time can be forgotten in complete involvement in study. Is it hard then to believe that life itself is found best when it is lost?

Life is found not by being saved but by being lost—lost in some deeper concern than selfishness. To save life is to lose it. To lose life is to find it. To hold on to what one has with jealous anxiety is to lose all. To share what one has with eager joy is to find more than one could ever hope for.

We have already noted the amazing story of Albert Schweitzer. He gave up all that he had as a masterful organist and as a brilliant scholar to go to the heart of Africa as a medical missionary. But in Africa he *found* more than he would ever have known had he stayed at home. His name is one of the first that comes to mind when we think of great personalities of our time. When a nineteen-year-old student was writing about the needs of Europe and the hopes for the future, he wrote that the best hope for the culture of Europe "is not in any part of Europe. It is in a small African village and it belongs to a man in his eighties." * Wherever life has been found through being given up, the name of Schweitzer is likely to be mentioned.

In the Bible there are many accounts of persons who have found themselves through giving themselves. Chief among these is Jesus. And next is Paul. Who would have believed that to give up his place of power and prestige and to endure continuous hardship would be the way to find his life!

■ Set goals for your study of this chapter as suggested on pages 15-16.

■ One person read aloud the Scripture passage of Paul's hardship (2 Corinthians 11:24-27). Follow this by unison reading of his affirmation about life and power (2 Corinthians 4:7-12).

The list of Paul's hardships is truly impressive:

Five times I have received at the hands of the Jews the forty lashes less one. Three times I have been beaten with rods; once I was stoned. Three times I have been shipwrecked; a night and a

day I have been adrift at sea; on frequent journeys, in danger
from rivers, danger from robbers, danger from my own people,
danger from Gentiles, danger in the city, danger in the wilderness, danger at sea, danger from false brethren; in toil and hardship, through many a sleepless night, in hunger and thirst, often
without food, in cold and exposure (2 Corinthians 11:24-27).

There is never the slightest hint that Paul ever regretted
giving up his old life of comfort and security. Instead, his
writings are filled with affirmations about a life of power.

But we have this treasure in earthen vessels, to show that the
transcendent power belongs to God and not to us. We are afflicted in every way, but not crushed; perplexed, but not driven
to despair; persecuted, but not forsaken; struck down, but not
destroyed; always carrying in the body the death of Jesus, so that
the life of Jesus may also be manifested in our bodies. For while
we live we are always being given up to death for Jesus' sake, so
that the life of Jesus may be manifested in our mortal flesh. So
death is at work in us, but life in you (2 Corinthians 4:7-12).

There is no question that Paul found himself in the very
act of giving himself so freely.

■ Read silently S/R, 100 and 101. Following the reading discuss
these questions: How can our confidence in God become strong
enough for us to make such affirmations and undergo such suffering for our faith? How do we try to justify to ourselves the ways
we avoid suffering for our faith?

OTHERS FIRST

Archibald realized that his life with Imogene had given
him a new perspective. By putting her needs ahead of his
own, he had discovered so much satisfaction that his own
needs seemed less urgent. It was first as a husband and then
as a father that Archibald began to appreciate the New Testament idea of finding your life by being willing to lose it.
It wasn't that he didn't have his own needs. They just seemed
to be met better when he put the needs of his family first.
The more room he gave to others, the more he discovered
for himself.

A self-centered life has no room for others. When Maggie
cries out to Quentin in *After the Fall,* "You should look at

127

me . . . like I *existed* . . . ," * she is protesting against being crowded out of her husband's life. He treats her like a piece of furniture to be used for his own convenience, but she wants to be a person who matters to him. The whole play centers around the question of whether or not Quentin can ever really love anyone. He realizes that until he can give himself in love to someone else, there isn't much of a future for him.

The two Sauls in the Bible struggle with the question of love of self as opposed to love of others. Saul, the king of Israel, ends his life with a sad declaration: "I have played the fool" (1 Samuel 26:21). When he should have been concerned about the things of his kingdom, he had instead spent his time in foolish attempts to destroy his rival. His personal jealousy was of more importance to him than giving leadership to his nation. Saul of Tarsus, on the other hand, could look back over his life with an affirmation. He had learned to live, not for himself, but for the new Christian faith. He no longer lived for himself; he lived for Christ and for all who were followers of Christ.

To give oneself to another is essential for Christian maturity, but it is not easy to accomplish. One of the favorite themes of the contemporary theater is the difficulty in establishing real intimacy, especially in marriage where it is so greatly desired. Arthur Miller gives a vivid picture of an empty marriage in *After the Fall* (in *After the Fall*, Quentin is married twice: first to Louise, second to Maggie). The complete inability of lawyer Quentin to sense his wife's needs is revealed as Quentin and Louise talk together. Quentin knows that something is radically wrong, but he fails to sense his responsibility for the condition.

■ Display the teaching picture "Quiet Evening at Home" (Resource Packet, item 10). See the Leaders' Guide. Two persons read aloud the dialogue below between Louise and Quentin from *After the Fall*. (To be used with the next procedural suggestion, page 129.)

Quentin. "In seven years we had never had a meeting. Never, never what you'd call . . . a meeting."

Louise. "We don't seem . . . *married*."

Quentin. "We?"

Louise. "You don't pay any attention to me."

. . . .

Quentin. "You mean like Friday night? When I didn't open the car door for you?"

Louise. "Well, that's a small thing, but it's part of what I mean, yes."

Quentin. "But I told you; you always opened the car door for yourself."

Louise. "I've always done everything for myself, but that doesn't mean it's right. Everybody notices it, Quentin."

Quentin. "What?"

Louise. "The way you behave toward me. I don't . . . exist. People are supposed to find out about each other. I am not all this uninteresting, Quentin. Many people, men *and* women, think I *am* interesting."

Quentin. "Well, I—. I—. I . . . don't know what you mean."

Louise. ". . . You have no conception of what a woman is. . . ."

Quentin. "But I do pay attention—just last night I read you my whole brief."

Louise. "Quentin, you think reading a brief to a woman is talking to her?"

Quentin. "But that's what's on my mind."

Louise. "But if that's all on your mind what do you need a wife for?"

Quentin. "Now what kind of a question is that?"

Louise. "Quentin, that's the question!"

Quentin. "What's the question?"

Louise. "What am I to you? Do you . . . do you ever *ask* me anything? Anything personal?"

Quentin. "But Louise, what am I supposed to ask you? I *know* you!"

Louise. "No. You don't know me. . . ." *

As long as Quentin treats Louise as if she doesn't exist, there is obviously no sense of intimacy. It is not enough for Quentin to lose himself in a legal brief. And to lose himself in a person like Louise seems more than he can do.

■ In the whole group discuss these questions: In this dialogue, what did Louise do? Why did she do it? How does her action compare with Jesus' teaching in Matthew 5:38-42? How can you make a man like Quentin aware you are alive? Should you try? Is such an attempt "putting others first" or putting yourself first?

129

To be sure, not everyone is capable of real intimacy. When Arthur Miller describes Linda, Willy's wife, in *Death of a Salesman,* he notes that Linda is aware of "the turbulent longings within" Willy. They are "longings which she shares but lacks the temperament to utter and follow to their end." * An even more dramatic statement of the inability to develop intimacy is found in Alan Paton's novel of South Africa, *Too Late the Phalarope.* The setting of this book is the Union (now Republic) of South Africa where the tensions between whites and Negroes were, and continue to be, so great. It is the story of a white police lieutenant who brings disgrace and ruin on his family by entering into an illicit relationship with a Negro girl. His aunt had sensed the agony he was going through before disaster struck. She condemns herself for not having forced herself to break through the barriers that he had erected.

> . . . He spoke hard and bitter words to me, and shut the door of his soul on me, and I withdrew. But I should have hammered on it, I should have broken it down with my naked hands, I should have cried out there not ceasing. . . . [but] *I held,* in the strange words of the English, *I held my peace.**

The aunt realizes too late that her nephew needed someone to help him to struggle with the dark emotions in the depth of his being. He needed to give himself in intimacy to someone who could help him to sort out his feelings. (*S/R,* 102.) But his hard and bitter words, spoken to cover the anguish of his heart, only drove everyone away.

OPENNESS FOR INTIMACY

Both Archibald and Imogene had had to learn to be open with each other. Imogene had received more training because her whole family had been so open. Marriage, however, was different, because no one can just walk away from marriage problems. Problems had to be worked through or nothing about marriage was any good. It wasn't easy, but both Imogene and Archibald discovered that by being more open about their feelings with each other, they were better able to handle their feelings with others. The closeness they were experiencing in their marriage made closeness in other relationships more possible.

Every teacher hopes a feeling of closeness will develop in his classes. Learning takes place more easily when teacher and student feel close to each other. A common mistake teachers make is to assume that new ideas can be grasped easily by the student, when the student has little background on which to build. But until the teacher understands the student's difficulty, little real learning can be expected. When the students are adults, it becomes all the more important for closeness to develop, because adults bring a wide variety of experiences that can greatly enrich the material under discussion. Unless the experience is communicated, however, it can easily be ignored.

The kind of openness needed for intimacy in marriage is also described in Paton's *Too Late the Phalarope*. Pieter, the police lieutenant, wrote a letter to his wife when she was away from home. He said in the letter what he was unable to say to her directly.

> . . . Perhaps one day when you are convinced, and know that my love of your body is part of my love of you yourself, and when you are no longer afraid of it, and accept it truly, and know that such love is no enemy, then perhaps I shall tell you more about myself, for you do not know it all. And if I knew your love was sure for ever, I should not fear to tell you, in fact I should wish to tell you. Then our love would be complete, and nothing would be hidden by one from the other. . . . Then I would be in heaven, and safe from all the dangers I told you of, and the angers and ugly moods. . . .*

Pieter tried to tell his wife of his inner questions and of his angry, ugly moods. He tried to involve himself with her at a deeper level, but she either couldn't hear his plea or was afraid to hear it. She wrote back:

> The long part of your letter I cannot answer fully now, but we shall talk about it when I get home. . . . As for these dangers, I think you imagine them, and they are not there at all.*

131

Like Linda in *Death of a Salesman,* Pieter's wife was unable to follow her husband into the deeper parts of his being. She made light of his inner problems. And of course she never did talk about "the long part" of the letter. His reception of her answer is dealt with in a paragraph consisting of a single sentence: "And he sat and read her letter with a face of stone." *

■ Individually read to yourself Pieter's letter to his wife and her reply on page 131. Whether you are a man or a woman, imagine now you are the wife. Write on a 3 x 5 card what you might say in reply to a letter like Pieter's. Let someone collect the unsigned cards, keeping them face down, shuffle them, and give one to each person for reading aloud. Be sure everyone realizes this procedure will prevent his or her reply from being identified. Let someone then read aloud S/R, 103.

Psychologist Carl Rogers writes at length about the need for intimate sharing if any kind of growth in depth is to result. He cites a young woman whose marriage had turned sour. Rogers had been counseling with her and had encouraged her to be more open with her husband even to the point of sharing some of her indiscretions. Finally, after a particularly bad evening together, the young woman told her husband about her feelings—her loathing of her hypocrisy and of her shallowness and of her inferiority feelings. (S/R, 103.) She wrote to Rogers to tell him about her husband's response.

". . . He was very accepting of the things I had done. . . . We *talked, discussed,* and really got down deep into so many of both our feelings. . . ."

"Now, I'm wondering—have you known all along that that was the only thing I could do to bring Bill and me closer? That that was the one thing I kept telling myself wouldn't be fair to Bill. I thought it would ruin his faith in me and in everyone. I had a barrier so big between Bill and me that I felt he was almost a stranger. . . ." *

It is not only between husband and wife that intimacy is needed. Let me share with you an experience with my own parents. I had prepared an autobiography to read in a professional gathering and decided to share it with my parents. Included in it was reference to an episode in my life in which I had disagreed vigorously with my parents. I had written somewhat critically of them. When in reading aloud I came to this portion, I was tempted to omit it but decided to share it anyway. There followed one of the best discussions I ever had with my parents. In talking of our tensions we came closer, I think, than we had ever been before. I have been particularly glad for those moments, because my father died soon after, before I could see him again.

The reason for trying to be open with others is that only through genuine openness can relationships of intimacy be developed. One way of thinking of this kind of relationship is in terms of dialogue. A dialogue involves two people, each of whom gives something of himself, invests something of himself, in the relationship. In dialogue, each person treats the other person as a human being to be cherished and not as a thing to be manipulated. In the picturesque terms of philosopher Martin Buber, the ideal relationship is spoken of as "I-Thou" rather than "I-It." An "It" is an animal or thing. (Look up the definition of "it" in a dictionary.) "Thou" is the pronoun (now out of use but helpful in seeing Buber's distinction) by which a *person* is addressed.

Each person is approached as a very special individual, as a "Thou." One of the chief characteristics of the I-Thou relationship is that each person reveals himself to the other as an authentic individual. The only way in which I-Thou dialogue can be established is through intimate sharing on the part of each. (*S/R*, 104, 105, and 106.)

■ Divide the class into groups of three persons. Let all groups be composed of men or women only. Discuss these questions: What are some possible reasons why Pieter's wife shut him off from expressing his deeper feelings? What are some times when we treat persons in similar fashion? Why do we do this? What happens to us and to them when we thus cut them off? (See *S/R*, 104 and 105.)
■ Read *S/R*, 106. What are the implications of the love of God as expressed here in your study group? your home? your work?

SAVING LIFE BY LOSING IT

Archibald disliked leaving his life open to attack. He knew that he gave the impression of having the answers, of having life well in hand. Often if he kept quiet, people thought he had things worked out. The temptation was always there to play it safe. But it never worked very well with Imogene. Perhaps it was because she knew him so well and loved him anyway. He could see how easy it would be to keep his defenses up most of the time. But he knew, too, that there wouldn't be much thrill in that kind of life.

To save one's life is rather easy. The will to live is very strong in any living thing. Any efforts at protecting life have this life-urge. To build protective barriers to provide safety from possible danger sounds like common sense. And so walls are built to shut men out. And life is made safe and secure, free from danger.

There is one major problem in life that is "safe." It loses its meaning. Had Jesus played it safe, there would be no Christian church today. Had Paul looked to his own safety, he would have given up before even starting on his first missionary journey. Martin Luther took a stand against the abuses of the church. John Wesley lost face in his own church for insisting on ordaining ministers, but his spiritual awakening saved England from a bloody, political revolution. Nurse Edith Cavell, in charge of a hospital in Brussels, Belgium, in 1915 when German troops occupied the city, assisted two hundred allied soldiers to escape into Holland. She lost her life but is remembered as a martyr who counted her own life as unimportant if others could be saved. King Christian of Denmark saved the lives of countless Jews from Nazi persecution in World War II by wearing a star of David on an arm band. He allied himself with all the Danes who were Jews.

It has never been popular to find life by losing it. The testimony, however, is overwhelming that meaning is found not in safety but in danger. The late President Kennedy liked to quote Dante that "the hottest places in Hell are reserved for those who, in a time of great moral crisis, maintain their neutrality." * It is generally safe to be neutral, but the issues of life, whether personal or international, are never solved by neutral spectators.

In his autobiographical account of life in a prisoner-of-war death camp, Ernest Gordon has a chapter entitled "Miracle by the River Kwai." The miracle that took place was a turning from death to life. Gordon experienced it in his own life, and he found evidences of the same miracle throughout the camp. The movement developed as stories of individual self-sacrifice began to circulate among the prisoners. One such story was about Angus McGillivray who was from Gordon's company.

As was the custom in his unit, Angus had a special pal, a "mucker" with whom he shared or "mucked in" everything. Angus' mucker became so ill under the terrible conditions of starvation diet and jungle diseases with no medicines that death seemed a certainty. But Angus was determined that his mucker would live. Gordon reports the story as it was told to him when he himself was being nursed back from near death.

> "Someone had stolen his mucker's blanket. Angus gave him his own. Every mealtime Angus would show up to draw his ration. But he wouldn't eat it. He would bring it round to give to his friend. Stood over him, he did, and made him eat it. Going hungry was hard on Angus, mind you, because he was a big man with a big frame. . . . Perhaps you know the end of the story. . . . The mucker got better. Then Angus collapsed. Just slumped down and died." *

When Gordon asked what the doctors reported as the cause of death, the answer was clear: "Starvation . . . complicated by exhaustion. He had mucked in everything he had —even his life." * In the days that followed, the story of Angus' sacrifice spread rapidly within the compound. It had "fired the imagination," * causing a stirring in the minds of many of a new feeling for each other, a new example to follow.

In the fighting, in taking the place that is needed, sometimes life is lost. But in the losing something even more worthwhile is found! The apostle Paul puts it in these terms: "None of us lives to himself, and none of us dies to himself. If we live, we live to the Lord, and if we die, we die to the Lord; so then, whether we live or whether we die, we are the Lord's" (Romans 14:7-8). We might add, "In such a life we find meaning!" (S/R, 107.)

■ Look at the series of cartoons, "The Foam Rubber Cross" (Resource Packet, item 11). Many Methodists rejoiced when they learned that the hymn, "The Old Rugged Cross," would be in the 1966 Hymnal (read the hymn, number 228 in the new hymnal). Yet the cartoons suggest that the perfect symbol of "faith" in our time is "The Foam Rubber Cross." Consider the hymn's symbolism: an old dirty cross, an emblem of suffering and shame, despised by the world, bloodstained, a place of death. Compare this with the improved cross, gold-plated, technological, luxurious, beautiful, and decorative. Which kind of cross has more power to lead us from death toward life? What acts of self-giving in our lives show that the Old Rugged Cross is really dearer to us than the new Foam Rubber Cross?

■ Look at the picture of a Mother's Hands scrubbing (Resource Packet, item 7d). Let someone read the story of the mother who scrubbed floors to win her son's freedom (S/R, 107). Then let this be a question left with the group to think about: Do we really have to go this far?

■ Close with the "Prayer of Saint Francis" (Resource Packet, item 3).

■ How will you prepare for the next session?

NOTES ON CHAPTER 8

Page 126: Quoted by Norman Cousins, "What Matters About Schweitzer" (editorial), *Saturday Review,* September 25, 1965, page 32. Used by permission.

Pages 127-28: Arthur Miller, *After the Fall* (Viking Press, 1964), page 103. Copyright © 1964 by Arthur Miller. Used by permission of the publisher.

Pages 128-29: *After the Fall,* pages 30-31. Used by permission.

Page 130: Arthur Miller, *Death of a Salesman* (Viking Press, 1949), page 12. Copyright 1949 by Arthur Miller. Used by permission of the publisher.

Page 130: Alan Paton, *Too Late the Phalarope* (Charles Scribner's Sons, 1953), page 1. Used by permission.

Page 131: *Too Late the Phalarope*, page 136. Used by permission.

Page 131: *Too Late the Phalarope*, page 137. Used by permission.

Page 132: *Too Late the Phalarope*, page 137. Used by permission.

Page 132: Carl Rogers, *On Becoming a Person* (Houghton Mifflin Company, 1961), pages 316-17. Used by permission.

Pages 134-35: John F. Kennedy, *Profiles in Courage* (Harper and Row, Memorial Edition, 1964), page 11. Used by permission of the publisher.

Page 135: Ernest Gordon, *Through the Valley of the Kwai* (Harper and Row, 1962), pages 102-3. Copyright 1962 by Ernest Gordon. Used by permission of the publisher.

Page 135: *Through the Valley of the Kwai*, page 103. Used by permission.

Page 135: *Through the Valley of the Kwai*, page 104. Used by permission.

Genesis 32:24-32
Jacob wrestles to receive a blessing. (*S/R*, 108.)

Genesis 28:10-22
Jacob dreams of God's presence.

(*Read these selections in your Bible*.)

9

□□□

OUR DEEPEST DESTINY

The day's work was almost over. Activity in the office picked up as five o'clock approached. Archibald was as glad as the rest that he could stop work, but he knew he would have to take some work home with him. Nobody told him he must, but his own sense of responsibility prodded him. No matter how the others felt, he could not enjoy leisure until his work was done. He felt a responsibility toward the company he worked for. He knew that he had found himself in this job and that nothing less than faithful performance would satisfy him. It was a matter of faith-ful-ness, of keeping faith with the best that he knew. A major reason for his concern with the church was that through the church he was beginning to understand what the best in life for him really was. His relationship with the church kept forcing him to ask himself, "What is the will of God for me in my work?"

■ *As you arrive at your place of meeting, check the assignment chart for specific preparation to be made before the session begins.*

139

There comes a time in everyone's life when he has a choice to make. For some this moment of decision is dealt with gradually over a period of time through many little decisions, all of which point in one direction. For others, the moment comes as a crisis with the future depending on the choice made. The choice is one of handling life or of being handled by life. It is one of carrying or being carried. It is one of serving or being served.

This moment of decision comes most commonly in young adulthood, but for some it comes much later in life. It can come at any point in life, but when it comes it marks the entrance into maturity. One of the most important marks of maturity is the willingness to accept responsibility for how life is lived. No longer is blame placed on unwise parents or on unfortunate circumstances or on bad advice. The mature person accepts responsibility for the consequences of his acts. (S/R, 109.)

Like so many of the biblical narratives, the Genesis record about Jacob is a timeless story of faithlessness and its results. Until the moment of self-discovery in all-night wrestling with an unknown opponent at the River Jabbok, Jacob's life was the story of one event of deceit followed by another. By taking advantage of his brother, Esau, in a moment of weakness and by cheating his father, Isaac, in his old age, Jacob secured advantages for himself. However, the pattern of deceit that Jacob began followed him as his father-in-law cheated him, his wife deceived her father, and his sons deceived their new neighbors. Jacob could not stop the train of events he had set in motion, but he could face up to his own problems. In the all-night encounter at the River Jabbok, he set his own life in order.

Jacob's all-night wrestling with an unknown man is the dramatic way of telling of an inner battle between the worst in him and the best. Paul wrote about the same contest: "I do not do the good I want, but the evil I do not want is what I do" (Romans 7:19). *The Three Faces of Eve* is the clinical case history of the contest within a sick patient. Here there are three parts struggling for control within a woman's personality. Anne Frank wrote in her diary of an inner battle: "I have, as it were, a dual personality." * When the impulse for self-advantage struggles for control with the impulse to relate positively with others, the contest is present in a person's life. Until this contest is resolved, there is little hope for finding any meaning in life. To find oneself as a responsible person is a prime requirement of maturity. (S/R, 110.)

■ Set goals for your study of this chapter as suggested on pages 15-16.

INDIVIDUAL UNIQUENESS

Being a father was a tremendous experience for Archibald. When he arrived home, the younger children would run to the door and jump into his arms. And Imogene would stop her work in the kitchen to give him a warm kiss. They all treated him like someone special. They made him feel unique. No one else could ever take his place. But it also meant that something special was called for from him. No one else could ever fill his shoes. It was up to him to carry his share of the load in his own special way.

When Holga in *After the Fall* says, "I think one must finally take one's life in one's arms, Quentin," * she is stating a basic truth. As long as someone else is expected to give direction to a person's life, there is little hope. Holga says in an earlier line: "Quentin, I think it's a mistake to ever look for hope outside one's self." * Hope is to be found, not by depending on someone else but by finding inner resources. Once this fact is recognized, the groundwork has been laid for accepting responsibility for choices.

A further question needs to be asked. What does it mean to find inner resources? For the Christian, inner resources are discovered when one's life is in tune with God's will. It is not the individual by himself who finds direction for his life. It is the individual who does his level best to bring his life in harmony with God's will and then gives himself in trust to whatever life brings who finds the deepest meaning. Holga's point is that one cannot find direction for someone else. The Christian goes beyond Holga to assert that without a world view that sees all of life under God there is little hope for meaningful direction for anyone. But when one accepts responsibility for how his life will be lived and centers his life in a search for God's will for him, the future becomes very bright. *(S/R,* 111.)

In his autobiographical story *Through the Valley of the Kwai,* Ernest Gordon tells of how he came to accept responsibility for what would happen to him. He tells of overhearing two medical men discussing his state of health. They spoke of malaria, dysentery, beriberi, unidentified blood infection, and the loss of the use of his legs after diptheria. Their conclusion was that "the only thing left is to let him have a decent end." * As Gordon puts it, "The death sentence had been pronounced on me by experts." * But he didn't die. A part of his recovery was due to the untiring efforts of Tom Rigden who built him a private hut to which he was moved from the death house. A part of it was due to Dusty Miller who washed the sores on his legs and tended him like a mother with a baby. But a large part of it was due to Gordon himself. He tells of his conversation with himself in which he decided to get out of the death house, even though he had been written off as hopeless.

> The atmosphere of the Death House was anti-life, the atmosphere of decay, of the potential "to be," ebbing away.
> "You're part of this," said Reason. "There is no escape. . . ."
> "The battle between life and death goes on all the time," I said to myself. "Life has to be cherished, not let go. I have made up my mind. I am not going to surrender."
> Then I asked myself, "What do I do about it?"
> It was a voice other than Reason that replied,
> "You could live. You could be. You could do. There's a purpose you have to fulfill. You'll become more conscious of it every day that you keep on living. There's a task for you; a responsibility that is yours and only yours."
> "Good enough," I said to myself. "I'll get on with it." *

142

The crucial part of Gordon's conversation with himself came in the decision to "get on with it." It was his fundamental faith that persuaded him to face up to life. His decision was similar to that of Jacob who decided to wrestle with his problems until he reached an answer. He would not let go until, struggling with his own inclinations and with his understanding of God's will for him, his better nature won out. His decision, made as the dawn was breaking, was to stake his life on God. Like Jacob, Gordon listened to the voice of faith when the voice of reason counseled giving up. (*S/R*, 112.)

■ After each person has read silently at least one of the *S/R*, 109 through 112, let one person read aloud Ernest Gordon's conversation within himself. Then in small groups compare his experience in the death house with that of Jacob at Bethel (*S/R*, 108) and Jesus in Gethsemane (Luke 22:39-46), in the following ways: (More than one group may deal with each question.)

Groups A: What was the basic decision each man made?

Groups B: What appears to have been the basis for the decision made by each man?

Groups C: What recent decision of yours is comparable to Ernest Gordon's saying to himself, "I'll get on with it, then"? Or Jesus' saying, "Thy will, not mine, be done"? Or Jacob's resolve to return home?

The philosopher-psychologist William James tells of reading an essay dealing with man's freedom to make choices. His response to the essay was to make the decision that he could control his own life. He puts the decision this way: "My first act of free will shall be to believe in free will." * This decision came after James had been struggling with poor health. He could easily have given up and resigned himself to the life of an invalid. But instead, like Gordon, James made a decision for life.

A present-day psychiatrist, Eric Berne, has developed a whole philosophy of treatment around the idea of man's capacity to make choices. He says that every chronologically grown person can function like an adult but many do not. Instead, when people are confronted by problems, they react as they did as children or as their parents reacted. To put it in another way, every person has within him a parent, an adult, and a child, and in each situation he decides which one will dominate. (S/R, 113.)

Eric Berne insists that a person finds himself as he refuses to allow the parent of the past to dictate his action and as he denies childlike expression in situations calling for adult response. He believes there is a time for the parent to hold forth, as when adherence to principle is called for. He believes, too, that childlike spontaneity is the basis for imaginative creativity and welcome naturalness. He reminds us that much of our thinking about religion is the result of the residue of childlike ideas and that adultlike thinking needs to take over in all areas of life. His major point, however, is that appropriate behavior can be called forth.

Although Berne writes without any concern about the Christian faith, his point of view is implicit in Christianity. A man is free to allow his whole being (parent, adult, and child) to come through. What Berne omits is the standard by which appropriateness for behavior is determined. The Christian faith provides the standard. It is by seeing all of life through the life and teachings of Jesus that what is appropriate (as parent, adult, or child) becomes clearer. (S/R, 114.)

PERSONAL RESPONSIBILITY

As Archibald put his papers into his brief case, he thought about his feelings of responsibility for doing the work. He knew his feelings had something to do with his religion. Going to Sunday morning worship didn't always have very much meaning for him. Just going to church, however, reminded him of God's claim on his life. Not that he would ever put it that way. When several of his friends teased him about his interest in religion, he could always pass it off with some wisecrack, but it really wasn't a joking matter with him. He knew that the best part of himself was related to his religion. Without faith it would be easy to live for himself. (S/R, 115.)

The question of personal responsibility touches almost every area of life. How responsible is the older person for the education of children who are not his own? How responsible is the majority to see to it that a minority group has access to decent housing? How responsible is anyone for the conditions that encourage delinquency? How far is a powerful nation responsible for the welfare of the less powerful? (*S/R*, 116.)

The Bible is full of references to personal responsibility. The prophet Nathan did not hesitate to point the finger of responsibility to David when he had schemed to get rid of Bathsheba's husband. Jacob thought he could escape facing the consequences of his acts, but his later life was filled with deceptions for which he could blame only his own example. When Jacob's sons deceived him by selling his favored son, Joseph, into slavery, telling him that Joseph had been killed, they were only continuing the pattern he had established. To the question asked by Cain, "Am I my brother's keeper?" (Genesis 4:9), a clear answer was given in the ministry of Jesus. No one is his brother's keeper, but everyone is his brother's brother.

Shortly after World War II, Arthur Miller wrote a play called *All My Sons*. This play deals with the question of personal responsibility. It is the story of a successful, small businessman named Keller whose sole purpose in life was to build a good business to leave to his two sons. During the war Keller made airplane engines for the Air Force. By some error, one hundred and twenty cracked engine heads were produced. The defect was covered up and the engines were sent out. After twenty-one planes were lost, the defect was traced to the shop where they were made. Keller managed to pass the blame on to his foreman who went to jail for it. As the play develops, it becomes apparent that Keller is really the guilty one. His son, Larry, had been killed in the war. Chris, the one son left, is trying to understand what happened:

Keller. "You're a boy, what could I do? I'm in business, a man is in business, a hundred and twenty cracked, you're out of business; . . . I never thought they'd install them. I swear to God. I thought they'd stop them before anybody took off."

Chris. "Then why'd you ship them out?"

Keller. "By the time they could spot them I thought I'd have the process going again, and I could show them they needed me and they'd let it go by. But weeks passed and I got no kick-back, so I was going to tell them."

Chris. "Then why didn't you tell them?"

Keller. "It was too late. The paper, it was all over the front page, twenty-one went down, it was too late. They came with handcuffs into the shop, what could I do? Chris . . . Chris, I did it for you, it was a chance and I took it for you. I'm sixty-one years old, when would I have another chance to make something for you? . . ." *

Keller tried to convince himself that being a responsible parent was enough. A letter that had been kept by Larry's fiancée brought Keller to face the facts. Larry had told in the letter of reading in the papers about the imperfect engines for which his father had been responsible. Larry's response had been to take his plane out and fly it into a mountain. The twenty-one pilots lost due to engine failure were like brothers to Larry. As Keller put it: "I think to him they were all my sons." * It wasn't enough to try to provide security just for his own two boys.

For Jesus, the ties of family loyalty were important but never absolute. When his mother and his brothers sent for him, he sent back the answer: "Whoever does the will of God is my brother, and sister, and mother" (Mark 3:35).

Chris, the surviving Keller son, is tempted to compromise, to see responsibility in a very narrow sense. After all, his father's intentions were good! In the end, however, Chris helps his father to face up to the thing that must be done. But it is too much for Keller. As the family thinks Keller is getting dressed to turn himself in to the authorities, he kills himself.

■ Let two persons read as dialogue the biblical story of David and Nathan (2 Samuel 12:1-10) ; then let the same two read the dialogue between Keller and Chris on page 146. After both readings are completed, let the readers tell how they felt during the second reading in comparison with their feelings during the first reading. In the total group discuss the question: What parallels do you see between the guilt of David and Keller and the courage of Nathan and Chris? What are some of the words or slogans we use to excuse our avoidance of personal responsibility? How can we become more aware that we are doing this? Where do we get the courage to call the hand of others, as Nathan did to David and Chris did to his father? Why should we?

In a strange way, Christian living makes some people more responsible while it makes others less. One of the common fallacies is to neglect to make this distinction. Some of the most scathing denunciations of religion have come from those who criticize the negative results of what is properly seen as neurotic religion.

Some people divide their lives into compartments in the name of religion. The result is that the insistent claims of God on all of life are completely overlooked. Such persons often deceive themselves by strict observance of religious practices without any application of religion to other areas of life. Some of the most monstrous acts in history have been committed by people who thought of themselves as deeply religious. The dream of Jacob in which he saw himself related intimately with God, even as he pursued deceitful ways, is a good illustration of how one's life can be compartmentalized. It wasn't until the all-night wrestling at Jabbok that Jacob realized he had failed in a religious sense.

Methodism has tried to keep personal piety permeated by social reform. (S/R, 117 and 118.) A large part of the secret of power in Methodism is due to the combination of these two factors. It is all to the good that we have insisted on both a personal responsibility for living the good life and a sharp sensitivity to the challenge of God to every area of life. The Lordship of Christ involves both redemptive and prophetic roles. (S/R, 119.)

■ In the whole group, discuss these questions: When we seem to feel a conflict of responsibility between God's will, the church's call, the family's need, and the job's demands, on what basis can we work to resolve the tension? What standards for decision do *S/R,* 115 through 119 suggest to you?

THE LARGER VIEW

As Archibald left the office, he was aware of the many relationships that formed his life. Being a part of his company was one, of course. Being a father was another. Being a citizen, a responsible member of his community and of his nation, was a third. Being a churchman and a member of the larger world-wide Christian community was still another. Each of these relationships gave form to his life and provided opportunities for finding meaning. They placed demands on him, too, but he wouldn't have chosen to drop any one of them. In a sense, these larger relationships called forth the best in him. He found himself in responding to these calls.

In thinking of the larger relationships to which he was responding, Archibald was facing outward. He was recognizing that there is a close relationship between what a person is and what he gives himself to. Wholeheartedness is the quality of the truly healthy person. In whatever direction he moves he goes as a whole person. His wholeness is in a large part due to the completeness of his response. Jesus stressed the sense of completeness when he spoke of the first great commandment: "You shall love the Lord your God with *all* your heart, and with *all* your soul, and with *all* your mind" (Matthew 22:37, italics mine).

It is not enough to have religious interests in life. No meaning in life comes necessarily out of following a religious pathway. Religion provides meaning in life only when it brings a complete response, when it becomes the supreme organizing influence in a person's life. Jacob was obviously a religious man, even to the point of dreaming about God (Genesis 28:10-22). But it was not until he put a concern about his relationship to God central in his life, in the all-night struggle at Jabbok, that religion brought meaning to him.

It is always instructive to discover what concern is foremost in a person's life. Gordon Allport tells of the explorer Raold Amundsen whose whole life was focused on arctic exploration.* The dominant concern throughout his lifetime was this interest that had taken form in his teen years. Nothing was permitted to stand in the way of trips to the arctic regions—flying over the North Pole, seeking a passage through the ice around the North Pole, eventually discovering the South Pole, giving up his life in rescuing a less successful explorer. He not only found a meaning for his life in this interest, but the arctic explorations became the supreme organizing factor in his life. His life could never be understood without taking into account where he was going. Unlike some psychologists who concern themselves only with the past, Allport cites Amundsen to remind us of the strong pull of the future. The commitments in a person's life play a large role in determining what kind of life it will be.

A less successful explorer was Captain Robert Falcon Scott. Amundsen got to the South Pole before Scott did. But Scott's diary found after his death in the Antarctic is a testimony to heroism and to commitment. Cherished in a glass case in the British Museum, the diary is opened to the last page where labored writing in pencil tells of the last hours. In a letter written about the same time to James Matthew Barrie, Scott wrote:

> "My dear Barrie: We are pegging out in a comfortless spot, feet frozen, no fuel and a long way from food, but it would do your heart good to be in our tent, to hear our songs and cheery conversation." *

At another point in the letter Scott writes that they knew they were taking risks, that they had no cause for complaint, that they wanted to show the world that Englishmen know how to die! Even at the point of death, their concern was not for themselves. Their lives were lived in broader relationships!

One reason that Arthur Miller is a great playwright is that he sees his characters related to the larger concerns of life. In

After the Fall, at the very end of the play Quentin is sum-marizing what he had discovered about himself and about life. He talks of forgiveness. As Christians, we can hardly think of forgiveness without thinking of Jesus. We recall how he encouraged forgiving not seven times but seventy times seven and how he spoke from the cross: "Father, forgive them; for they know not what they do" (Luke 23:34) . The idea of forgiving enemies is a Christian concept. Forgiveness stretches our thinking, moves away from self-centered living into living for others. When Quentin thinks of the hateful feelings that anyone knows so well in his heart, he responds in terms of forgiveness.

> "The wish to kill is never killed, but with some gift of courage one may look into its face when it appears, and with a stroke of love—as to an idiot in the house—forgive it; again and again—forever?" *

Quentin puts a question mark where the Christian faith puts an exclamation mark. Forgiveness is an essential in human life because it pulls a person out of self-centered liv-ing and requires a relationship with others, a relationship that is informed by the Christian ideal.

When Ernest Gordon wrote of the miracle taking place in the death camp at the River Kwai, he spoke of it in terms of a sense of relatedness to God.

> We were learning what it means to be alive—to be human. As we became more aware of our responsibility to God the Father, we realized that we were put in this world not to be served but to serve. . . . There was a general awakening. Men began to smile—even to laugh—and to sing.*

Men could sing because they began to sense that their lives were lived in a relationship with a larger dimension, one which called on them to reach out in service.

■ Have on display the photo, "Man in a Cage" (Resource Packet, item 12) . In small groups discuss: What kinds of experience and feeling give us the sense of being "caught in a cage"? What existing conditions in our own lives do the bars represent? How does the promise of God's forgiveness give us hope of release and full acceptance? What else, if anything, do we need to fulfill our destiny—what must *we* do?

Many people consider William James to be America's greatest psychologist. Although he wrote at the turn of the century, his writings are being republished and read today in paperbacks. He talked quite openly about God. "We and God," he wrote, "have business with each other; and in opening ourselves to his influence our deepest destiny is fulfilled." *

Gordon Allport chooses not to use the term *God* at all because the term has so many distorted images. (*S/R*, 120.) Instead, he tells about the concern of religion with *supreme context*, a context large enough to be inclusive of all of life. Everyone, he says, actually has a context, a framework, within which he lives his life. When that context becomes large enough to include every aspect of life, it is the supreme context. He defines religion in a way that many non-religious persons can accept.

> A man's religion is the audacious bid he makes to bind himself to creation and to the Creator. It is his ultimate attempt to enlarge and to complete his own personality by finding the supreme context in which he rightly belongs. *

The larger relationships of life make for meaning in two ways. On the one hand, they provide a source for power. Archibald derives strength from his position as a member of the firm, as a father, as a churchman. He counts on these relationships to provide support when he needs help. He depends on them for encouragement and reinforcement. But, on the other hand, the larger relationships in life require service. They demand attention. They exist because of devotion and commitment. By living in touch with the larger relationships of life a human being lives as all living things do—appropriating and releasing power that they do not create but which they use.

Finding oneself and thus finding meaning involves selecting the relationships that will mold one's life. As William James puts it, "The seeker of his truest, strongest, deepest self must review the list carefully, and pick out the one on which to stake his salvation." * For the Christian the one on whom to stake one's salvation, the one who provides the supreme context for life, is Jesus of Nazareth. In Paul's words, "In him [Christ] all things hold together" (Colossians 1:17).

As a modern theologian expresses it, Jesus Christ is "the hinge of history." * He is the hinge in the sense that in him the past and the present come together. Christ was in the past and is in the present. He was a historical person walking the streets of Jerusalem, and he is a present reality in lives open to him. He is the hinge in the sense that to live in his spirit is to give a new dimension to both past and present, to fill both with new meaning. In him the past is redeemed, no matter how awful it has been, and the future is filled with promise.

■ Pray together the "Prayer of Saint Francis" (Resource Packet, item 3).

■ How will you prepare for the next session? (See the suggestion for a report on adult education opportunities, page 159.)

NOTES ON CHAPTER 9

Page 141: Anne Frank, *The Diary of a Young Girl* (Doubleday and Company, 1952), page 281. Copyright 1952 by Otto H. Frank. Used by permission of the publisher.

Page 141: Arthur Miller, *After the Fall* (Viking Press, 1964), page 24. Copyright © 1964 by Arthur Miller. Used by permission of the publisher.

Page 141: *After the Fall* (this quote does not appear in the Viking Press edition but appears in other editions of this play).

Page 142: Ernest Gordon, *Through the Valley of the Kwai* (Harper and Row, 1962), page 86. Copyright 1962 by Ernest Gordon. Used by permission of the publisher.

Page 142: *Through the Valley of the Kwai,* page 87. Used by permission.

Page 142: *Through the Valley of the Kwai,* page 89. Used by permission.

Page 143: William James, *The Letters of William James* (Little, Brown and Company, 1926), Volume I, page 147.

Page 146: Arthur Miller, *All My Sons* in *Six Great Modern Plays* (Dell Publishing Company, 1958), pages 419-20. Copyright 1949 by Arthur Miller. Used by permission of Viking Press.

Page 146: *All My Sons* in *Six Great Modern Plays,* page 432. Used by permission.

Page 149: Gordon Allport, *Becoming* (Yale University Press, 1955), page 49.

Page 149: Quoted by G. Bromley Oxnam, *Facing the Future Unafraid* (Fleming H. Revell Company, 1944), page 12. Used by permission.

Page 150: *After the Fall,* page 128. Used by permission.

Page 150: *Through the Valley of the Kwai,* page 145. Used by permission.

Page 151: William James, *The Varieties of Religious Experience* (Random House, 1963), page 507. Used by permission.

Page 151: Gordon Allport, *The Individual and His Religion* (Macmillan Company, 1950), page 142. Used by permission.

Page 152: William James, *Psychology: Brief Course* (Henry Holt and Company, 1900), page 186. Used by permission.

Page 152: Carl Michalson, *The Hinge of History* (Charles Scribner's Sons, 1959), page 173. Used by permission.

Exodus 3:1-12
God calls Moses to leadership. *(S/R, 121.)*

2 Corinthians 5:13-21
Christ brings a new creation.
(Read these selections in your Bible.)

10
□□□
GROW OR DIE!

While the children chattered at the supper table, Archibald realized how much they were learning and how fast they were growing. One of the boys was talking about the most recent launching of a satellite and was wondering what happened to the burnt-out rocket that had launched it. It reminded Archibald that his youngsters knew so much more about the space age than he did. He couldn't even follow his daughter in her junior high math! But the daughter was explaining to her brother how the rocket burned itself up. Archibald caught Imogene's eye and they smiled to each other across the table. They would have to grow some to keep up with their children. This was no time to settle down into comfortable ruts. There was too much going on in the world around to settle back into middle-aged ways. This was the time to keep growing.

Very few battles of life are concluded with a once-and-for-all victory. Most of them have to be fought again and again.

■ *As you arrive at your place of meeting, check the assignment chart for specific preparation to be made before the session begins.*

Even the most routine life requires constant choice and constant decisions. A man decides when he will get up, what he will wear, what he will eat for breakfast, what words he will speak, what mood he will express. Life does not stand still. It persists in presenting man with choices to be made.

Choice, however, presents opportunities for growth. One of the common issues of maturity centers in the struggle between allowing habit to dictate life or choosing new and creative ways of acting. A great advantage of travel is that habitual patterns are challenged by new ways of living. My daughter is spending a year in Switzerland as a part of the International Christian Youth Exchange (ICYE) program. She is discovering at firsthand how different life is in a Swiss family. Invite a foreigner into *your* home and discover how many of your customs are strange to him! Many people are unaware how routine their lives have become, how closed to new ideas, how fearful of change. (*S/R*, 122.)

One of the great stories of growth is the call of Moses in the Old Testament (Exodus 3:1-12). From life as a shepherd, Moses was called to the life of leading the Israelites out from slavery to Egypt. According to the account, as he was taking care of his sheep in the wilderness, he saw a bush on fire but it was not burning up. He turned aside to see what this strange sight meant. In doing so he received a call from God to assume a position of leadership among the Israelites in Egypt. Many persons would not have been curious enough even to explore the strange occurrence. But Moses did explore it and was led to a new vocation. The burning bush story is more than an account of the call of Moses. It is also the story of the struggle that any person well established in life faces when some new factor calls for a change. It is the story of how reluctant anyone is to leave the comfort of accustomed ways to brave the uncertainties of the unknown. But if life is to have meaning, growth must be continuous.

KEEP GROWING

Imogene felt very proud as she looked across the table at Archibald. He was more attractive to her now than he had ever been. Somehow he was more alive, more alert, more interesting. Imogene knew that the training sessions Archibald was participating in at work had helped as had the church study group. She could almost see Archibald's mind stretching to grow up in his religious thinking. It made her realize that she needed to do some stretching, too. Archibald had been encouraging her to pick up her music again and perhaps she should. She realized that she had fallen into bad habits of uncritical judgments. She really hadn't done much hard thinking for some time.

Growing is hard. Parents find they have to struggle with their children who do not want to grow up. Teachers can expect a certain amount of dislike from students, since teachers demand growth, and no one really welcomes growth. Growth creates anxiety. It means venturing away from the familiar and comfortable. It means risking the uncertainty of the new in place of feeling secure in the certainty of the old. (S/R, 123.)

Moses did not want to change. He tried to excuse himself from making any change. When God called him in the wilderness, he was well established in life. He had already tried more than one type of work. In Egypt he had lived a life of luxury in the palace until in a moment of anger he had killed an Egyptian taskmaster. His flight from Egypt must have been difficult, and life as a shepherd was certainly different from life at court. But he had made the adjustment, had married and settled down into a simple, routine way of life. It is very clear that he did not welcome a change. He did not want to respond to God's call to new opportunities.

Resistance to changing one's way of life is very common. Ernest Gordon tells of being asked by men in the death camp on the River Kwai to give leadership in a class that wanted to study the Christian faith. The sergeant who approached him put the issue quite simply:

> "We've all seen the worst there is—right? Now we feel there must be something better—somewhere. So we want to have

another go at this Christianity—to find out if it's absolute
'dingo' or not. . . ."
"We got to wondering if maybe there isn't something in this
Christianity business after all—something we haven't understood
aright in the past." *

The sergeant, as spokesman for the men, asked Gordon to
lead the group. Gordon's immediate response, like that of
Moses, was to beg off. "But why me?" he asked. "Surely there
must be others who could do the job much better than I."

This was the same kind of reluctance that Moses knew,
and it is the same kind of hesitation that nearly anyone has
when he is called upon to provide leadership. The Bible is
filled with the stories of men who tried to flee from a call to
a special ministry. The stories of Gideon, Samuel, David,
Elisha, Amos, Isaiah, Jeremiah, Jonah, and Paul all tell of
hesitancy before a call. (S/R, 124.) For the biblical characters the call was directly from God. For Gordon the call
came through a sergeant, but in a very real sense it was from
God, too. It was a call to make full use of his abilities.

Gordon was not allowed an easy escape. The sergeant insisted stubbornly that the men knew whom they wanted.

"They think you're right for it. . . . For one thing, they know
you're a fighting soldier. For another, they hear you've been to
university, so you ought to know something about Christianity." *

Gordon was "floored" by the request. "I wanted," he wrote,
"to refuse immediately." * But he didn't. As he talked with
the sergeant he discovered that the sergeant, who had been
a good athlete, had organized and trained a team of men to
massage paralyzed legs to try to restore them to health. The
sergeant's example made it hard to refuse his request. And
so Gordon agreed.

"All right, . . . I'll try to give them the real 'dingo.' But mark
you, I won't promise that anything I can say will have any meaning for them." *

What he had to say to the men eventually brought meaning to his own life. He found meaning as he sought to stimulate growth in the thinking of the men.

■ Set goals for your study of this chapter as suggested on pages 15-16.
■ Two persons read aloud as dialogue the story of Moses' call
(Exodus 3:1-12). Then each person read silently *S/R, 124.*
■ In small groups, discuss these questions: What do you understand
by the words, "God's call"? What are some typical ways men resist
God's call? Share experiences of your resistance to God's call to
change or grow. How did your attitude compare with that of Moses
or Ernest Gordon? What was the outcome? Why do you feel this
experience was God's call?
■ Brainstorm (list as many possibilities as you can think of quickly,
without evaluation or discussion) : What kinds of help could members of this group offer to persons imprisoned either literally or
socially or mentally? Set up a committee to formulate a plan for
possible courses of action. Let the committee investigate and report the plan at the last session of this unit of study.

Gordon's acceptance of leadership in a class in religious
inquiry marked a kind of rebirth in his life. The new direction that his life took led to theological study and finally
to the position of Dean of the Chapel at Princeton University. It was like being born again into a new life.

Most professional people pass through a crisis in middle
age. They make a decision, consciously or unconsciously, to
settle down or to keep growing. The temptation is to settle
into orthodox ways, religious or psychological or some other.
The alternative is to accept the challenge to grow, to remain
open to new, creative development.

■ In the whole group, hear a report on the topic: Opportunities in
the community that are open to us for mental, emotional, or professional growth, such as clubs, film festivals, lecture series, or
adult education courses. (Consult your annual conference board of
education for data.) Who in our group is participating? How can
this learning be shared and used for God by the group?

A NUDGE TOWARD GROWTH

Life had not been all rosy for Archibald and Imogene.
Their three children meant more to them because they had
lost a baby. They had tried to make life safe for their children by choosing a house on a dead-end street where traffic
would be light. But a delivery truck, in an unguarded mo-

ment, killed their toddler. At the time their grief had seemed overwhelming, but out of it they had grown. They had learned of the community of suffering—the fellowship, the sense of closeness, that draws together people who have suffered. They had come to recognize that life is in the hands of God and that there is no such thing as absolute security. They had grown together, too, as they supported each other in their tragedy.

This is the same thought behind Paul's words in Romans 5:3-4: "We rejoice in our sufferings, knowing that suffering produces endurance, and endurance produces character, and character produces hope." The constructive use of suffering as a spur toward growth has always been a part of the Christian faith. When Paul asserts that "in everything God works for good" (Romans 8:28), he includes suffering and tragedy. (S/R, 125.)

A positive response to undeserved suffering always evokes admiration. Harry Emerson Fosdick, the great preacher of the Riverside Church in New York City, tells the true story of a girl with the unlikely name of Mercy Goodfaith.* Living in an orphanage, unloved and unwanted, this ten-year-old girl was an unhappy, sickly, ill-tempered, ugly, little hunchback. But one day a woman came to the orphanage looking for a child that no one else wanted. When she saw Mercy Goodfaith, she declared: "That's the child I'm looking for." Thirty-five years later an investigator of homes for county orphans reported on a home that was remarkable for its atmosphere. The children were remarkably happy in a spotlessly clean home. After supper the children gathered around the matron in the living room to sing while one of the older girls played an organ. They pressed as close to the matron as they could. The smallest child sat on her lap. Others leaned against the matron as they sat on the floor at her feet. One of the boys lovingly stroked the hem of her dress. Obviously the group adored her. She was an ugly hunchback. Her name was Mercy Goodfaith. Out of her suffering she had found her life of service in relieving the suffering of others. She was a living testimony that "in everything God works for good." (*S/R*, 126.)

Just as suffering can be a spur to growth, so can failure. One of the best documented stories of failure is the life of Abraham Lincoln. At the time he was nominated for the presidency, his career had been dogged with failure. At twenty-two, after seven years of hard work, he lost all he had saved when the sheriff's sign was nailed across the door of his bankrupt country store. Two years later his partner died, saddling him with another business failure and with debts that troubled him for the next fifteen years. At thirty he started a surveying business. He borrowed a horse and instruments, only to lose the instruments to creditors. The one girl he really loved died and his heart followed her to her grave. The woman he married was more interested in his success than in his happiness. He was elected to Congress for two short terms, but he failed to gain re-election. Twice he was defeated in attempts to gain a seat in the Senate. He had expected to be the presidential nominee of his party, but on the very eve of the convention his hopes crashed. Nearly everything he had attempted had failed. In 1841 he wrote of himself: "I am now the most miserable man living. If what I feel were equally distributed to the whole human family, there would not be one cheerful face on earth." *

Yet this man who had known failure so intimately became the president of the United States. He takes his place among the great spiritual leaders of the world. Confronted by the cause of saving the Union, his personal difficulties seemed unimportant. Lincoln's capacity to rise above failure, to be spurred on by failure, grew out of his deep sense of being used by God. When he left Springfield, Illinois, to take up the presidency, he spoke these farewell words: "Without the assistance of that Divine Being who ever attended him [Washington], I cannot succeed. With that assistance, I cannot fail." Relying on God, he rose above failure.

In some ways Moses was a study in failure. Until the response to the call of God the day he saw the burning bush, Moses had little to show for his life. The act of pride in Egypt, which eventually kept him out of the Promised Land, made his early life a failure. To bury his genius under a shepherd's coat was certainly no mark of success. But failure didn't stop Moses, either. He grew out of failure when he accepted God's cause, one that was worth giving himself to. Adventuring with God changed his life drastically.

■ Three persons read aloud: *S/R,* 125 and 126, and 2 Samuel 12:15b-23. Then in the whole group discuss: Why is the faith of a suffering person so impressive? How valid do these expressions of faith (in the readings) seem to you?

A recent best seller describes women in America as having failed to make use of their potential creativeness. Betty Friedan in *The Feminine Mystique* describes how women in our country tend to stress their biological function to the exclusion of all else. By focusing on the nursery and kitchen, women have killed off any real creativeness in their lives and so have condemned themselves to a life of discontent and dissatisfaction, Friedan believes. She presents a challenge:

> There is no way for these women to break out of their comfortable concentration camps except by finally putting forth an effort—that human effort which reaches beyond biology, beyond the narrow walls of home, to help shape the future. Only by such a personal commitment to the future can American women break out of the housewife trap and truly find fulfillment as wives and mothers—by fulfilling their own unique possibilities as separate human beings.*

Betty Friedan puts the next move in the woman's hands. If the woman finds no meaning in the routine of life in which she feels caught between diapers and the dishpan, then she needs to be searching for deeper meaning.

Not only women feel caught in routines. A common mood for the middle-aged person is expressed by Quentin in *After the Fall* when he says: "I seem to be hung up." * C. G. Jung, the Swiss psychiatrist who specialized in working with middle-aged people, cites one of his patients as being typical when he said: "I am stuck." * Jung believes that no middle-aged person finds real satisfaction in life until he makes use of all his capacities. He sees the person in middle age as a different person from what he was in young adulthood. He feels "stuck" because the goals that seemed so important in early adulthood now have lost their appeal. (S/R, 127.) The young man is deeply involved in establishing himself in a job, in finding a wife and raising a family, and in acquiring a home and a car or two. The middle-aged man (thirty-five and older), however, has different interests. He begins to ask questions about the "rat-race" toward success. He becomes disillusioned about the struggle for material things. He tends to become more contemplative, to be more interested in developing a philosophy of life. His interest in religious values becomes more pronounced. He tries to become more of a whole person.

Women, on the other hand, are seen by Jung as moving in the opposite direction. The breakup of some marriages after fifteen or so years can be understood in terms of the changing needs of both women and men. For the most part, young women in our culture are preoccupied with children and home. Their time is taken up with the nursery and the kitchen. The result is that many of their other talents lie unused. The middle-aged woman who feels caught suddenly realizes how little of herself she has made use of. She senses that she has denied her own talents. She begins to desire more involvement in life, more participation in the world outside her home, more voice in how life is lived. She wants to become more of a whole person. The crisis of middle age nudges her toward growth. She wants to feel related to all of life in a more meaningful way.

■ Let one person read aloud S/R, 127. Then individually engage in an act of self-examination. Betty Friedan challenges women to "fulfill their own unique possibilities as separate human beings." This challenge is valid for every person. Dare you answer these questions?

1. Am I maintaining my physical capacities in ways appropriate to my age, or am I neglecting my body?

2. Am I using my mental capacities by reading books and articles with new ideas and by seeing stimulating movies and television programs, or am I just staring at the same old westerns and quiz programs?

3. Am I using my emotional capacities by feeling with others in their need, or am I shutting myself off from people so I'll never get hurt?

4. Am I using my senses to become aware of new sights, sounds, and smells, or am I denying myself all forms of beauty?

5. Am I using my travel potential to go new places and have new experiences, or am I keeping to old familiar ruts?

6. In short, am I really loving God with all my mind and soul and heart and strength?

Some men and women create their own meaning. Some deliberately place themselves in positions of danger in order to feel involved in life. (S/R, 128.)

■ Read S/R, 128. In what ways does this act fulfill Jesus' teaching in Matthew 25:31-46 and his words, "Greater love has no man than this, that a man lay down his life for his friends" (John 15:13)?

CHRISTIAN GOALS

It was never easy for Archibald to put into words just what his faith meant to him. He had always liked the roll call of the faithful in the eleventh chapter of Hebrews, however, because it gave a sense of direction to history. He thought of his faith in those terms—not as giving specific directions about how he should live his life but as pointing him in the direction that could give meaning to all that he did. It was this part of his faith that had helped him to keep going through the tragic death of his child. He couldn't understand the death, but even in his questioning he was supported by a sense of movement. He was going somewhere. He wasn't just stumbling in the darkness. His life had direction to it, a goal toward which he was moving. He felt a sense of partnership with God and that made all the difference in the world. (S/R, 129.)

A great affirmation of the Christian faith is expressed in very simple words: "If any one is in Christ, he is a new

creation; the old has passed away, behold, the new has come"
(2 Corinthians 5:17). To be in Christ, that is to live a life
so directed by the spirit of Christ that one lives under the
control of Christ, is to grow into a new person. It is to be
so transformed that the result is not just a slight change but
is rather a complete transformation. (S/R, 130.)

It is written that Moses' face glowed after he was confronted by God on Mount Sinai. When Stephen was telling
the story of God's guidance of the children of Israel, his face
shone "like the face of an angel" (Acts 6:15). There is a
glory that shines from the faces of those who live close to
God. On one occasion my father, who was an Old Testament
scholar, had been translating the psalms from the Hebrew.
When he came down from his study to join the family, his
brother (my uncle) said that my father's face glowed like
those who had been in the very presence of God. There is a
radiance about those whose lives encounter the living God.
It is as if they have found their way to a source of power, the
wells of which never run dry.

C. G. Jung was quite explicit about the place of religion
in the lives of people who sought therapeutic help from him.

> ". . . Among all my patients in the second half of life—that
> is to say, over thirty-five—there has not been one whose prob-
> lem in the last resort was not that of finding a religious outlook
> on life. It is safe to say that every one of them fell ill because he
> had lost that which the living religions of every age have given
> to their followers, and none of them has been really healed who
> did not regain his religious outlook. . . .*

Many present-day novelists like William Faulkner and
present-day playwrights like Tennessee Williams write of
meaninglessness but have little to say about hope. They write
in the age of nuclear fission. They write of atomization of personality and of the dehumanization of man. They write of
an age of breakdown of moral standards, of absence of absolute values. Their writing makes it clear that without fixed
guideposts, man loses his sense of direction and eventually

his sense of identity. In describing the absurdity of much of man's life today, these writers are implying the need for rethinking the place of God in life. While appearing to be godless, they may prove to be the strongest impetus to a new search for the living God. (S/R, 131.)

Without God, without some all-encompassing unity, life does not make sense. To be human is to keep growing, to keep searching for greater meaning in life.

For Jesus there was never any question about the goal in life. A verse in John's gospel expresses his whole life view very clearly. "Knowing . . . that he had come from God and was going to God, [he] . . . girded himself with a towel . . . and began to wash the disciples' feet" (John 13:3-5). His whole life was a demonstration of service based on the love of God. He was very clear about priorities: first the love of God and second the love of fellow man. His statement of the great commandments is very pointed: "You shall love the Lord your God with all your heart, and with all your soul, and with all your mind. This is the great and first commandment. And a second is like it, You shall love your neighbor as yourself" (Matthew 22:37-39).

■ Listen to a panel or a resource person on this question: How can writers and artists who appear to be godless, but who show the absurdity of life without God, provide strong impetus to a new search for the real God? (See S/R, 131.) In preparation, you might agree as a group to see any movie currently being shown in your community or view any television show. After hearing the panel or resource person, discuss what you saw using the questions in the chart, "How to Discuss a Secular Film" (Resource Packet, item 13), as a guide.

■ Conclude with the "Prayer of Saint Francis" (Resource Packet, item 3).

■ How will you prepare for the next session?

NOTES ON CHAPTER 10

Pages 157-58: Ernest Gordon, *Through the Valley of the Kwai* (Harper and Row, 1962), pages 115-16. Copyright 1962 by Ernest Gordon. Used by permission of the publisher.

Page 158: *Through the Valley of the Kwai*, page 116. Used by permission.

Page 158: *Through the Valley of the Kwai,* page 116. Used by permission.

Page 158: *Through the Valley of the Kwai,* page 117. Used by permission.

Page 160: Compare Harry Emerson Fosdick, *On Being a Real Person* (Harper and Row, 1943), page 72.

Page 161: *The Collected Works of Abraham Lincoln* (Rutgers University Press, 1953), I, page 229. Used by permission.

Page 162: Betty Friedan, *The Feminine Mystique* (Dell Publishing Company, 1965), page 325. Used by permission of W. W. Norton and Company.

Page 162: Arthur Miller, *After the Fall* (Viking Press, 1964), page 4. Copyright © 1964 by Arthur Miller. Used by permission of the publisher.

Page 163: C. G. Jung, *Modern Man in Search of a Soul* (Harcourt, Brace and World, 1955), page 70. Used by permission.

Page 165: *Modern Man in Search of a Soul,* page 264. Used by permission.

'THE CRUCIFIXION," BY GEORGE BELLOWS, COURTESY THE ART INSTITUTE OF CHICAG

Daniel 3:8-25
Shadrach, Meshach, and Abednego stand against the king. *(S/R, 132.)*

2 Corinthians 4:7-8
Perplexed but not in despair.

(Read these selections in your Bible.)

11

□□

SAY YES TO LIFE

The last thing Archibald wanted to do was to leave home after supper to go to the hearing before the city council. He had never been one to involve himself in politics, and the questions about housing in the city had strong political overtones. But the real reason he didn't want to go was deeper than that, he knew in his heart. He just didn't like conflict. In spite of his personal feelings, he knew he had to go. Whether he liked it or not, he was a responsible citizen. What he thought did make a difference. If housing regulations needed to be established so that minority groups could be protected in their efforts at finding decent housing, then he wanted to be there to put in his word. When property rights were thought of as more important than human values, then something was really wrong. Much as he didn't want to bother, he knew that he had to face the facts. After all, people do count more than things!

■ *As you arrive at your place of meeting, check the assignment chart for specific preparation to be made before the session begins.*

169

On his eighty-eighth birthday, Robert Frost wrote down his thoughts about life. Looking back over the years he wrote: "You've got to be sweeping and you've got to be pointed. You've got to come out somewhere. . . ." * This was the poet's way of saying that a man has to take a stand. He has to hold to a position that is broad enough to deal with great issues and yet is pointed enough to lead to specific action. To be able to see clearly for the long pull and at the same time be able to make clear-cut decisions in the present is one of the goals of Christian maturity.

The Old Testament story of Shadrach, Meshach, and Abednego is a dramatic account of men whose lives were lived by principle. They showed what it takes to "come out somewhere." The guiding principle of their lives was loyalty to God. When they were commanded by a foreign king to worship an idol, they refused. They were certain that the God whom they worshiped would help them to find a way out, even though death in a fiery furnace threatened them. There is more to the story, however, than a statement of this position. In a defiant assertion they took a particular stand: "But if not, . . . we will not serve your gods." Even if their God did not help them escape, they would still hold to this position. It is the "but if not" that wrote the names of these three men among the heroes of history.

Dag Hammarskjöld, the late secretary-general of the United Nations, is a present-day hero. Hammarskjöld was a genius at finding a way out when every possible pathway seemed blocked.

Hammarskjöld's orientation as a practicing Christian was to take seriously Jesus' words in the Sermon on the Mount, "Take . . . no thought for the morrow . . ." (Matthew 6:34, King James Version). What this meant for Hammarskjöld was that existence had meaning and life moved toward a goal, even though the meaning and the goal were not always evident. "Taking no thought" meant for him faith in the future. When Hammarskjöld was killed in a plane crash, he was carrying out his mission for the United Nations. There was no question about his ability either to face life or to find meaning in it. (*S/R,* 133.)

■ Set goals for your study of this chapter as suggested on pages 15-16.

■ Read aloud or silently *S/R,* 132, 133, and 134.

HANDLING WHATEVER COMES

As Archibald guided Imogene to a seat in the city council chambers, he felt the familiar anxiety that always came when he wasn't sure of himself. He knew that before the evening was over he would be making some people angry with him. But he knew he had confidence about being able to handle whatever would occur. He believed that his position was the right one and so he felt strengthened to hold to it. It wasn't like standing alone. It was like standing with all the forces of good—and that made him feel strong. (*S/R,* 134.)

Mrs. Miniver is the story of a family whose faith was very secure. In the days of the London blitz, even though bombs were shaking the foundations of their house, a power greater than the bombs was present. It was the same sense of power that the Danish people knew during the war when, locked out of their churches by Nazi order, they gathered outside the churches on the steps and sang of a fortress that could not be taken: "A mighty fortress is our God, a bulwark never failing" (*The Methodist Hymnal,* 20).

Life *can* be faced. This is one of the strongest affirmations of the Christian faith. It is expressed in a biblical verse that has been spoken of as the best possible psychological advice: "Having done all, . . . stand" (Ephesians 6:13). (*S/R,* 135.) Throughout the Bible this assertion is continually made. When a person who seeks God's will has done all that he can, then he can stand fast in the confidence that his strength is reinforced by God. This was the confidence of Shadrach, Meshach, and Abednego and was the source of their power. The same thought is expressed in one of the great benedic-

171

tions of the church: "Now to him who is able to keep you from falling . . ." (Jude 24). A person's faith does not keep him out of danger. When a person confronts danger, there is a way out.

■ Hold a Quiet Meeting for a few minutes. With the group in meditation, anyone says what he feels led to say—not necessarily related to the previous speaker.

No situation is completely hopeless, even though it appears to be. A positive note is struck by Harold Russell in his autobiography which became the movie *The Best Years of Our Lives*. Russell was a sergeant in charge of a demolitions unit in World War II. In training for combat he lost both of his hands. Eventually he was fitted with two hooks that he learned to use very skillfully. His initial reaction was one of resentment when strangers would approach him to talk about his hooks. Finally, however, he recognized that they were only trying to be friendly. He tells of the day when he really resolved his feelings. In a Chinese restaurant a stranger had watched his eating with chopsticks. The man came over from another table and started a conversation.

"I was noticing," he said, "how well you manage those things."
"These?" I held up the chopsticks.
"No—I—er—mean those—" He swallowed hard and nodded at the hooks. "Well—*those*—"
"Oh! You mean, my hooks?"
He sighed with relief. It was obvious he had been embarrassed to call them by their right name.
"I couldn't help noticing how skilful you are with them," he said. "You can just about do everything with them, can't you, sergeant?"
"Everything," I said, grinning, "except pick up a dinner check." *

When he could make a joke over his disability, he had really arrived.

Russell learned to live with his handicap by putting it in its proper perspective. He wrote:

. . . It is not what you have lost, but what you have left that counts. Too many of us squander precious energy, time and courage dreaming of things that were and never can be again, instead of dedicating ourselves to realities and the heavy tasks of today. I think I can speak with some authority on this subject. I wasted many weary months trying to wishfully think back a pair of hands.*

■ Two persons read aloud as dialogue the scene from *After the Fall* (Resource Packet, item 14). In the whole group, discuss these questions: What difference do you see in the power of Harold Russell (pages 172-73) and Maggie (in the play) to face their disabilities? How, if at all, do we receive the power to accept responsibility for ourselves?

The existentialists write a great deal about death. (*S/R,* 136.) For them, the only one sure fact in life is death. Since everyone dies, sooner or later, how a person faces death is a concern for all. For some people, death is simply the last absurd fact in an absurd world. For others death is another incident that can bring meaning to life.

The poet Robinson Jeffers writes of a young woman who becomes alive as she faces death. He calls his poem "Where I." It tells of a young woman who discovers that she is about to die. The knowledge that death lies immediately ahead, however, does not destroy her. On the contrary, it transforms her. It helps her to grow. It helps her to see all things in a new light—"terror, pain, joy, the song." Facing death, she is more alive than ever before. (*S/R,* 137.) The reader of the Gospels gains the same impression about Jesus.

This young girl's outlook is not expressed in Christian terms. Nevertheless, it is fundamentally Christian. Paul Tournier, the Swiss doctor who combines religion and psychology so effectively, notes this emphasis:

Our attitude to life is always a reflection of our attitude to God. Saying "Yes" to God is saying "Yes" to life, to all its problems and difficulties—"Yes" instead of "No," an attitude of adventure instead of one of going on strike.*

The poet Robert Browning actually talks of facing death as an adventure. (*S/R,* 138.)

■ Read silently *S/R*, 136, 137, and 138, and the quotation from Tournier on page 173. In small groups discuss these questions: Do you believe that a person's attitude toward death is a reflection of his attitude toward God? Why or why not? How has someone you know found meaning in facing death or bereavement? How does the poem by Jeffers (*S/R*, 137) compare with your understanding of a Christian attitude toward death?

DISTORTING THE FACTS

Archibald knew that he could count on support from many of the people at the hearing. He knew, too, that others would be opposed, regardless of the facts that he presented. He tended to find facts to support his own prejudices and overlooked the facts that would make him question his point of view. He knew that he did this in his marriage even though he tried hard not to. Imogene was even less likely to pay attention to the facts. As with most people, her feelings really directed her thinking. But Archibald knew that the facts had to be uncovered and then lived with. However unlovely the facts were, they could not be escaped.

When Scarlett O'Hara in *Gone With the Wind* says, "I'll think of that tomorrow," it is easy to understand her mood. Some people find the facts so distasteful that they try to ignore them. Others will keep one set of facts separated from others as if in watertight compartments. If, for example, what one learns in science is in contradiction to what one learns in religion, some try to handle the problem by keeping the two areas separated. But the facts need not be evaded. They can be faced. They do not need to be pushed aside or overlooked or distorted. Whatever the facts are, they can be lived with.

In my work with theological students and their wives, I often find that marriages stay on a superficial level if negative feelings can't be faced. One couple considered divorce until the young wife asserted herself for the first time. She became a person in her own right, stopped playing the role of a child wife, and let her husband know how she resented his autocratic ways. He, in turn, expressed his unhappiness in finding himself married to a docile, colorless child who would do whatever he suggested. Their marriage was re-established on a much firmer footing with a minimum of help. They simply had learned to face the facts.

Often the facts get distorted. A French film maker produced a film called *Anatomy of a Marriage* that is really two films. One is written from the perspective of the wife and is called "My Days with Jean-Marc." The other, written from the husband's point of view, is called "My Nights with Francoise" and presents an entirely different picture. The same facts are seen as parts of two separate worlds. The wife sees her husband as a thoughtless, petty, little man whose jealous possessiveness of her is intolerable. She does not see him at all as he sees himself—a dedicated lawyer, deeply in love with his wife, his daughter, and his work but forced to give up his work with delinquent adolescents in the provinces because of his wife's desire to live in Paris. He sees her as a spoiled little girl who is unfaithful to him and inconsiderate of his wishes. He sees none of the love that she feels for him, does not see the tears that she sheds after he slams the door, does not sense the desperation that leads her to compensate for a spineless husband by seeking a career in advertising in the city. Each film presents a one-sided picture showing how little real communication was taking place and emphasizing how distorted the facts really were.

■ Let representatives from various occupations form a panel on this topic: "How persons in my line of work are tempted to distort the truth about their social standing, their finances, and the quality of their goods or services." After a few minutes turn to this question: Does our faith help us *face the facts* of our lives, or do we *use it as an excuse* to distort the truth—as by giving good-sounding reasons for what we do? Or do we use it in both ways?

Eric Berne, whose theory of Parent-Adult-Child has already been mentioned, cites a situation in which the facts are often confused. A husband and a wife are dressing for dinner. The husband says to his wife: "Do you know where my cuff links are?" * The wife is immediately confronted with a choice.

She can interpret the question as the question of a helpless child, in which case she will tend to respond in a parental way. She might then say: "Why don't you keep track of your own things? You're not a child any more." * Or she might interpret his question as a parental-like scolding to her and say in a childlike way: "You always blame me for everything." * Or she might hear his question as an adult who needs information and respond in an adultlike fashion that she doesn't know. Or she might say that she thinks they are in the top drawer of his dresser. The interpretation she places on his question determines the nature of her response. The fact of the matter is less important than how she responds to it.

■ Have someone prepared to present a reaction to *S/R*, 113. Try some spontaneous two-person conversations similar to the one on pages 175-76) , in front of the group. Then let the group decide whether the person who replies is speaking as a child, parent, or adult. What are some other ways of confusing facts? When are we most likely to act as a child? as a parent? as an adult?

A major goal of psychiatry is to understand what these barriers are in order that they may be removed. By seeking understanding, the psychologist avoids passing critical judgment. For example, when obnoxious behavior is observed, the psychologist is always interested in the reasons that lie behind the behavior. No one is obnoxious just to be obnoxious. By his disagreeable behavior a person is trying to achieve some goal, inappropriate as the method may be. The question the psychologist likes to ask is: "What's *really* going on here?" He likes to look behind the act to the meaning.

■ Bring and share newspaper clippings that report or show expressions of anger. Discuss: How can we find out what is *really* going on behind another person's hostility? What difference does it make in our reactions when we know why another person is angry?

CHRISTIAN HOPE

As the hearing began, Archibald sensed a kind of inner peace, even though he was quite uncertain about how things would go. He realized that his faith helped him to see things in terms of the long pull. Even if the hearing went against him, he felt confident that a solution to the problem could be found. He realized that this mood made him less arbitrary, more open to hearing the other fellow. He knew that his optimism about life was something rather new, something he had seen in Imogene but had made his own only through the study of his faith. He knew how fortunate he was to be able to face uncertainties without being upset. He knew that some of the people at the hearing were driven by a sense of desperation.

It is easy to give way to despair when everything seems to go wrong. Yet the opportunity to choose is always present. A mark of the human being is that he makes choices. One writer speaks of man as a "deciding being." By this he implies that the quality that distinguishes man from an animal is his power of choice. In the story of Shadrach, Meshach, and Abednego, lesser men would have despaired before the power of the king. But these men did not. With the dramatic flair of the Near East writer, the three men are depicted walking alive amidst the fire of the furnace. A fourth person was with them. How else could the writer have said that God was with them!

Dag Hammarskjöld's faith was more than the religion of his fathers, although it was that, too. In a very personal way he had made his faith his own. In the foreword to *Markings* (his diary), Hammarskjöld tells how he accepted his faith by an act of free choice even though his intellect could not wholly reconcile his philosophy with his religion. He gives a penetrating statement of how he sensed the need for belief in God to give direction to his life. (*S/R*, 139 and 140.)

■ Read *S/R*, 139. In pairs discuss these questions: From your study of this whole unit, how do you think one becomes able to say Yes to life? When, specifically, are you more likely to say Yes and when No? Why so?

■ Let someone read aloud *S/R*, 140. Then individually fill in this brief questionnaire. How concerned are you about the problems of people around the world? Here you may find some clues:

Yes__No__Uncertain__The United States should do all it can to help "underdeveloped countries" raise their standard of living.

Yes__No__Uncertain__The United States should open its doors to refugees whoever they may be.

Yes__No__Uncertain__Every person has an equal right to good housing, food, job, education.

Yes__No__Uncertain__Sending educational and medical missionaries to other countries is helpful.

Yes__No__Uncertain__Most of the really poor people around the world are poor mostly because they are lazy and really happy, if agitators don't stir them up.

Yes__No__Uncertain__I think every person has an equal right to his own views and an equal right to promote these views, whether or not I agree.

Yes__No__Uncertain__New nations should be allowed to determine their own policies and form of government and should be helped by stronger nations to do so.

After seeing your own reactions, do you feel you have a worldwide view or a smaller limit of concern? How can your circle of concern become more like God's circle of concern?

From many perspectives, disgust and despair result from a realistic appraisal of life. Much of the negative quality of present-day writers reflects this mood. But the late theologian Carl Michalson saw in this negativism a powerful ally to Christianity. He wrote:

> . . . The current though despairing revolt against all artificial meanings is a cultural event of great importance to the church because it documents in a secular way the Christian conviction that meaning is not humanly apparent. . . . *

As long as meaning is sought on the purely human dimension without any reference to the activity of God in history, the results will be only meaninglessness and despair. The negativism of much of today's literature reflects a culture that has sought centers of meaning apart from its God-centered tradition in the Hebrew-Christian faith.

No one has surpassed Paul's statement of the antidote to despair. He tells of perplexity but not yielding to despair, of persecution without a sense of being forsaken, of being struck down without a sense of being destroyed. His affirmation is declared in memorable words: ". . . We have this treasure in earthen vessels, to show that the transcendent power belongs to God and not to us. We are afflicted in every way, but not crushed; perplexed, but not driven to despair" (2 Corinthians 4:7-8). He finds the basis for courage not in man but in God. He can say: "So we do not lose heart. . . . Our inner nature is being renewed every day" (2 Corinthians 4:16). Because of God, there is hope. (*S/R*, 141.)

■ Read again 2 Corinthians 4:7-18, and *S/R*, 141. Why do you think the point is made above that expressions of despair and disgust in contemporary literature are powerful allies of the gospel because they demonstrate the truth of this Christian belief: meaning cannot be found apart from faith in God's activity in history? Is this belief part of your faith and hope? What are evidences of God's activity in history?

■ Conclude with the "Prayer of Saint Francis" (Resource Packet, item 3).

■ How will you prepare for the next session?

NOTES ON CHAPTER 11

Page 170: Quoted by Paul Boch, "The Search for Meaning," *Journal of the United Church of Christ,* November, 1965, page 7. Used by permission.

Page 172: Harold Russell and Victor Rosen, *Victory in My Hands* (Farrar, Straus and Giroux, 1949), page 151. Copyright 1949 by Harold Russell and Victor Rosen. Used by permission of the publisher.

Page 173: *Victory in My Hands,* pages 279-80. Used by permission.

Page 173: Paul Tournier, *The Adventure of Living* (Harper and Row, 1965), page 196. Copyright 1965 by Paul Tournier. Used by permission.

Page 175: Eric Berne, *Games People Play* (Grove Press, 1964), page 31. Used by permission.

Page 176: *Games People Play,* page 32. Used by permission.

Page 176: *Games People Play,* page 31. Used by permission.

Page 178: Carl Michalson, *The Hinge of History* (Charles Scribner's Sons, 1959), page 236. Used by permission.

Luke 19:1-10
Zacchaeus rediscovers community. (*S/R*, 142.)

Luke 15:4-7
The finding of the lost.
(*Read these selections in your Bible.*)

12

□□□

FINDING MEANING
THROUGH FAITH

Imogene did the driving as they left the hearing. Archibald was tired but happy. His left hand rested lightly on Imogene's shoulder, conveying by touch his feeling of closeness with her. He felt good about the hearing. The outcome was still uncertain, but he wasn't worried. Meanwhile, he would keep plugging for what he believed to be right. He was thinking through the next step as they passed their church building. The building was dark, but the outline of the sanctuary with its sharply pitched roof stood out boldly against the moonlit sky. He would be there for his breakfast study group in the morning—a group that had come to mean more and more to him. It wasn't that he had found answers to all the questions that bothered him, but to have companions in the search helped a lot. And the answers were coming, just as his love for Imogene was deepening and his feeling about life was broadening. He knew that he hadn't really found all the meaning he was seeking, but he was on the way.

■ *As you arrive at your place of meeting, check the assignment chart for specific preparation to be made before the session begins.*

Chiseled in the walls of the magnificent Thomas Jefferson Memorial in Washington, D.C., is a reminder of the need to change with changing times. Jefferson wrote: "Laws and institutions must go hand in hand with the progress of the human mind." Although he was thinking of laws of government, his advice is just as good for religion. The church needs constantly to seek new ways of expressing its faith. (S/R, 143.)

Throughout the pages of this book we have been studying attempts by men and women to express their search for meaning. Much of the searching goes on outside the church. Indeed, when Archibald MacLeish wrote a play called *J. B.*, based on the biblical story of Job, audiences in London rejected the play as unreal. One critic believed that the most objectionable line was the one spoken by J. B. (who plays the part of a modern Job) when he said: "I've always known that God was with me." Since many people have no such assurance, this line rings false in many ears.

Whether we like it or not, ideas about "God, mother, and country" no longer hold the power they did in the past. This fact is borne out by the "God is dead" movement, by disregard for aged parents, by the burning of draft cards. (S/R, 144.) Even in theological schools, familiarity with the Scriptures can no longer be assumed, and, for many, Bible reading and daily devotions are largely activities of the past. Yet the overthrow of cherished ideas and of familiar forms is not necessarily a bad thing. To find new ways of thinking and acting springing up within the church suggests a vitality that is indeed encouraging. Answers may no longer be clear, but the search is certainly going on.

How misguided a search for meaning can be is demonstrated in the story of Zacchaeus. Like many of the biblical stories, this episode in the life of Jesus is likely to lose much of its real meaning when too much consideration is given to the outward facts. The story says that Zacchaeus climbed a tree because he was short in height and that his problem centered in the fact that he was a tax collector. The importance of the story does not depend either on his size or on his position. The story is a significant one because it tells what goes on in the life of any person who is cut off from his group. Zacchaeus represents a man in isolation and as such is a good representative of many modern men. He tried to fill the emptiness in his life with wealth but it didn't work any better with him than it ever does with anyone else. Until he was restored to a relationship with his community, there could be no real satisfaction in his life.

MEANING CAN BE FOUND THROUGH FAITH

The breakfast study group at the church had become a genuine fellowship. It was much more than just another activity for Archibald. It had become one of the most important events in his life. He had found an acceptance in the group that he had never even dared to hope for. When his boss had not given him a promotion, he had shared with the group his sense of failure. They had been so understanding that he dared to share more of his feelings. He told them of his anger when his father had interfered in his family life. And he told them of his feelings of inadequacy when trying to discipline his children. They, in turn, had shared many of their concerns with him. As the men supported each other, they began to sense the deeper meanings of their faith. (S/R, 145.) Now Paul's words in Ephesians took on more meaning: "So then you are no longer strangers and sojourners, but you are fellow citizens with the saints and members of the household of God, built upon the foundation of the apostles and prophets, Christ Jesus himself being the chief cornerstone" (Ephesians 2:19-20). In their study and sharing together, the men of the breakfast group felt a comradeship that bound them together. But even more, it provided a common bond in their loyalty that reached beyond their group to Christ, the cornerstone of their faith.

Meaning for life needs to be discovered. It doesn't present itself but has to be sought after in faith. It is found in the normal patterns of life, in family living, at work, in study,

183

and in the daily routine. Jesus helped Zacchaeus to find meaning in his life in very ordinary ways. He called Zacchaeus down from the tree, invited himself into Zacchaeus' home, and shared a common meal. There was no special royal pathway to meaning. It came to Zacchaeus in the familiar moment of breaking bread together in the presence of someone who understood his loneliness, sensed the longing for relatedness, and made relationships possible. Feeling accepted, Zacchaeus found the best coming out in him.

There are some hints about how meaning is found. At least three steps can be pointed to, steps that are all related to faith but which do not start with faith. The first step is taken when the worst that life can bring is faced. To face despair is the beginning of handling it.

The late Paul Tillich was not only a very able theologian; he was also a talented critic of art and culture. He liked to refer to a painting by the artist Picasso as "a great Protestant painting." * It is Picasso's "Guernica," a large painting done entirely in black and white. It shows the total destruction of the little Spanish town of Guernica by Fascist airplanes. The painting shows the evil of war with human bodies torn apart, children killed, and animals destroyed. Tillich writes that Protestantism emphasizes man's inability to save himself. Man needs God's help in rising above his own inhumanity. He goes on to say why this is a great Protestant picture:

> The human situation in its conflicts should be expressed courageously. If it is expressed, it is already transcended: He who can bear and express guilt shows that he already knows about "acceptance-in-spite-of." He who can bear and express meaninglessness shows that he experiences meaning within his desert of meaninglessness. *

This is the first step, the one Picasso has taken—to face the depths of despair openly and courageously.

The second step is commitment. It involves taking a stand, making a decision, exercising a choice. (S/R, 146.) It is finding a clear sense of direction and then holding to it. It is the basic step in Christianity, the step that goes beyond secular orientations to life. It is the step that puts service to others ahead of satisfaction of personal needs. It is the step that Zacchaeus took when, instead of thinking of his own wealth, he thought of squaring his relationship with others. It is finding oneself by being willing to lose it for others. It is a willingness to undergo crucifixion, the dying to self, in order to experience resurrection, the birth of a new self. Quentin in *After the Fall* begins to sense that hope lies through forgiveness. Ernest Gordon finds himself as he provides leadership for others. Dag Hammarskjöld gives his life so that a new world order may be established.

The third step is one of action. Zacchaeus did not find meaning by talking about it. He found meaning in specific steps. He would repay whatever injustices he had done. He would act on his new resolve. William James insisted that man has a part in creating his own world. A mood is created by action. If you want to feel happy, then act happy. Action leads to feeling rather than vice versa. As one of his teachers put it: "Your experience is constantly transformed by your deeds." *

Jesus spoke to Zacchaeus in terms of action: "Make haste and come down . . ." (Luke 19:5a) . Note how often his challenge was to one of action. The words spoken to the rich young ruler were typical of his form of address: "Go, sell, give, come, follow." It is no wonder that the cross of Christ calls a person to action. If the cross is truly experienced, it requires taking a stand. (*S/R,* 147.) You can't be indifferent about the cross. It lays a claim on your life. Like any genuine symbol, it is oriented to action. (*S/R,* 148.)

■ Set goals for your study of this chapter as suggested on pages 15-16.

■ Show the filmslip, "Search" using the *second* script and record (Resource Packet, item 2) . Read the script if you have no projector. See the Leaders' Guide for suggestions for use.

■ Have three persons as a panel discuss the question: Why are these three steps so necessary a part of the search for a meaningful faith: Facing the worst life can bring; willingness to sacrifice one-

185

self; and action. (See *S/R,* 146, 147, and 148 as background material.)

MEANINGFUL FAITH REQUIRES RELATEDNESS

It had been a long day. Archibald was glad to see the lights of their home as Imogene drove down their street. He knew that his home could be a haven for him, a safe refuge, but it was more than that. It was a base to move out from. It was the testing place for Christian community, the place where forgiving love demonstrated its power. He sensed how much of his faith had its roots in his boyhood home. He had learned how much of Imogene's trusting attitudes had come from her home. He knew his children were forming *their* attitudes toward life around the family table, when they went camping, when they shared sorrow. He hoped his children would find in their family the basis for trust that would give them an optimism about life. He knew that their growth in faith was tied up with family relationships. And he knew that their life in the larger community would reflect what they had learned in their family.

The number of people who are lonely is absolutely astounding. *(S/R,* 149.) We have already seen how important it is that a person develop a sense of trust so that he can reach out to others trusting that he will find response. But we have also noted how hard it is for some persons to trust.

Zacchaeus was like that. Because the Jews hated tax collectors like him, he had been cut off from his own Jewish community. We can guess that his efforts at relating himself to others in his town had met with failure. He longed to be a part of his own group. But only Jesus saw the longing. Most people only saw that Zacchaeus had deserted them for the enemy. *(S/R,* 150.) When he climbed a tree in his eagerness to look in on what was happening, staying apart as an outsider, only Jesus recognized his loneliness.

■ One person read aloud *S/R,* 149 and 150. Then brainstorm (list without discussion all the points you can think of) : ways people shut themselves off from others; ways we attempt to overcome loneliness comparable to Zacchaeus.

One of my students reported on an insurance salesman who put into words the longing that many feel. In answer to the student's question, "What is an adult looking for?" he wrote:

Many of us are fearful and alone to a greater or lesser degree. We often feel that our problems are unique. As a result we pick up life by the heavy end. A deadening cycle begins. We feel rejected and put upon by a hostile universe. Rejection begets fear; fear suggests aloneness; loneliness hints at a greater distance between one's self and his fellow man. I guess that a cycle somewhat similar to this is just waiting to get a head start in all of us. When it does, it can make our lives literally something to be endured between terminals. Back to the question: What is an adult looking for? A sense of well-being, worth, meaning, the feeling of being at home in the universe; a sense of belonging.

It is significant that this salesman ends with the idea of being at home, not just in a group, but in the universe as well. In commenting on the Cain and Abel story, Harry Overstreet points out the fundamental truth in Cain's protest when he is told that he is to become "a fugitive and a vagabond . . . in the earth." Cain declares: "My punishment is greater than I can bear." * (See Genesis 4:8-16.) To have no niche in life, to be totally unrelated, is a living death.

■ *Discuss in four small groups:* Group 1: How true of people we know is the salesman's word of longing? (above). Has anyone experienced the cycle he describes? How can it be broken? Does it lie near the surface in all of us? Group 2: Does being a part of the church tend to make you feel more "at home in the universe," or more like an alien who doesn't really belong in the world? Group 3: How does this group help you find meaning in what you may become, as well as what you are now? Group 4: What larger concerns than yourself has this group helped you become related to? Share brief reports from each group with the whole group.

The Bible is clear; tragedy is not the last word. The good news of the Christian faith is that God reaches out to every man, accepting him not because he is deserving but because he is man. Whenever a man dares to face himself, even in the depths of guilt, God accepts him. Whoever dares to move out to his fellow man with compassion and forgiveness moves with God.

RELATEDNESS THROUGH COMMUNITY

The closeness that Archibald felt with Imogene was a part of his feeling of being at peace within himself. And both of these feelings were involved with his faith. But faith didn't come naturally to him. It had to be nurtured. It needed constant confirmation, constant reinforcing. (*S/R,* 151.) He needed his family, his neighbors, his study group, his fellow workers. He realized that being at peace with the world was a part of being related in meaningful ways with the people around him.

For most people, faith needs to be nurtured. The father who took his sick son to Jesus to be healed stated the matter clearly when he declared: "I believe; help my unbelief!" (Mark 9:24). To find a group that is accepting of a person as he is, is one of the great needs in any person's life. Belief is strengthened when unbelief, too, is taken for granted. An accepting group is a primary requirement for the nurture of faith. (*S/R,* 152 and 153.)

The church has a tremendous potential for demonstrating community. The story of a church that became a "community of forgiveness" has been told by William Hawley. Charles Farrow, a broker and a member of one of the blue-blood families of the city, was indicted on a charge of embezzling $15,000 from his firm. He pleaded guilty and was sentenced to two years in the state prison. As a member of the church vestry, his imprisonment left a vacancy. By church law, the vestry had to make a recommendation for filling the vacancy at the next meeting. One member of the vestry, however, urged that the vacancy be held open for the return of Farrow. He spoke of the need of the church to be a redemptive force in human life, of his feeling that somehow Farrow's sin was his sin, too. He reminded the vestrymen of the rector's sermon the previous Sunday. The sermon was based on the parable of the shepherd who left ninety-nine sheep to go out to look for the one that was lost. "If my analysis is a correct one," he concluded, "this story vividly describes what we as a parish have failed to do." *

The matter wasn't decided then because heated argument followed. Eventually it was decided to hold the vacancy open. On the day that Charles Farrow was released from prison, he found the rector and all the vestrymen waiting for him at the prison gate. They went together on the two-and-a-half hour drive to the church where they knelt together at the altar for Holy Communion. On the way the rector explained their decision to reconfirm Farrow as a member of the vestry:

> What became clear to us was that all these years we had been assuming that we were a church, when actually we were not. We had failed to recognize that a church is not a church until it is a community of forgiveness, and it cannot be a community of forgiveness until we first recognize and confess our human frailties, our pride in our self-sufficiency.*

This group came to recognize that true community starts with a common confession of shortcomings. It was natural to kneel together at the communion table. The service of Holy Communion includes the humble prayer of confession in which all worshipers admit their sins. It took an obvious sin to remind the others of their less conspicuous but nonetheless definite shortcomings. The final prayer of thanksgiving reminds the worshiper of what God has done for him. God has accepted him, unworthy as he is. (S/R, 154.) And God sends him forth to create the Christian community wherever he goes.

> ■ In the whole group, discuss the question: How near are we to the spirit of the vestry that became a community of forgiveness? (See also S/R, 1 and 152.)

In contrast to Hawley's story of the "Community of Forgiveness" is the practice described by James Michener in his novel *Caravans* of cutting off a man's right hand as punishment in a primitive, non-Christian culture for a severe crime.* Because only the right hand can be used to dip into the common dish at mealtime, the loss of the right hand meant virtual exclusion from society.

In the Zacchaeus story, wholeness and salvation are used almost as synonyms. When Jesus said to Zacchaeus, "Today salvation has come to this house," he might have said that Zacchaeus had been made whole again. Zacchaeus was restored to the Jewish community. Health and healing, another way of speaking of wholeness, came when the broken bonds of fellowship had been repaired. One of the delightful personal notes in the story is the way in which Jesus went about his ministry to Zacchaeus. He invited himself into Zacchaeus' home. He took the almost unforgivable step, in the eyes of the crowd, of inviting himself to sit at the same table with an acknowledged sinner. He demonstrated community rather than just talking about it.

Meaning came to Zacchaeus as it comes to anyone. It came when the broken bonds of fellowship had been restored. It came when personal wrongs had been righted. It came when loneliness had been penetrated and isolation had been overcome. It came when a loyalty to God took priority over all other loyalties. It came when a clear sense of direction gave a new focus for the future. It came when another life was opened to the spirit of Jesus of Nazareth. (S/R, 155.)

■ Hear the report from the committee appointed to find ways to help those in prison in some way. How can we demonstrate community, as Jesus did by taking the initiative with Zacchaeus? Complete the planning and assign responsibility.

■ Look at the card on which, in the first session of this study, you wrote an honest evaluation of the state of your faith. How has your faith (and your honesty) changed through this study? Prayerfully, revise your own evaluation.

■ Use the Christian Group Life Check List (Resource Packet, item 16). Select points to discuss for a final evaluation of your learning process.

■ Conclude with the "Prayer of Saint Francis" (Resource Packet, item 3).

Note

The author and the editors hope you have used the materials and suggestions of this unit freely. We hope you have taken more than a quarter for your study. If you do have time for another session before the second unit of Foundation Studies becomes available, we suggest you go back and try some of the procedures you omitted. Or read together some of the Selected Readings you missed, and some of the dialogues from plays. Or repeat some procedures that might have more meaning for you now.

NOTES ON CHAPTER 12

Page 184: Paul Tillich, *Theology of Culture* (Oxford University Press, 1959), page 68. Used by permission. Originally published in *The Christian Scholar,* December 4, 1957.

Page 184: *Theology of Culture,* page 75. Used by permission.

Page 185: Josiah Royce, *William James and Other Essays* (Macmillan Company, 1911), page 37. Used by permission.

Page 187: H. A. Overstreet, *The Great Enterprise* (W. W. Norton and Company, 1952), page 72. Used by permission.

Page 189: William N. Hawley, "Community of Forgiveness," *The Inter-collegian* (published by the National Student Councils of the YMCA and YWCA), October, 1953, page 12. Used by permission.

Page 189: "Community of Forgiveness," *The Inter-collegian,* October, 1953, page 14. Used by permission.

Page 190: James A. Michener, *Caravans* (Random House, 1963), page 291.